D1561007

Ocean Liners

Ocean Liners

Jonathan Forty & David Williams

PRC

This edition first published in 2001 by
PRC Publishing Ltd,
8-10 Blenheim Court,
Brewery Road, London N7 9NY

© 2001 PRC Publishing Ltd

ISBN 1 85648 607 9

Printed and bound in China

**PREVIOUS PAGE: The modern cruise liner *Royal Viking Sea*
docked in Edinburgh, Scotland.**

**RIGHT: From the previous generation of liners, the *Queen
Elizabeth*, which, with her running mate *Queen Mary*, established
the Cunard Line as the dominant operator on the North Atlantic
service.**

CONTENTS

ODUCTION

Introduction

"Enter the world of the ocean liner. See how a rudder 80 ft high, which weighs 101 tons, is easily moved by one hand, and the direction of its movement is shown on the captain's bridge and in the engine-room. The boilers of one ship cover an area of five acres. Funnels rise from the engine-room to a height of 180 ft.

"Think of ships with nine decks! It is well on half a mile's walk round the deck of such a ship from bow to stern and back. Deck space is equal to no fewer than eight football fields. The top of the hollow steel masts that carry the radio wires high above the funnels are 225 ft above the keel!

"These great vessels need large anchors and cables. The anchors weigh 151 tons each, and the cables are 1,800 ft long, made of great steel links.

PREVIOUS PAGE: *Emerald,* **operated by Thomson Holidays, carries 1,198 passengers on ten decks.**

BELOW: The *Wind Star* **is a smaller vessel that harks back to earlier days of ocean travel. Operated by Windstar Cruises it carries only 148 passengers.**

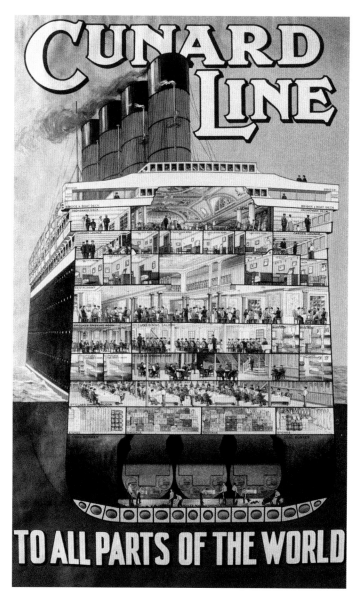

"On the foremast there is a crow's-nest 'look-out' and a 150,000-candle-power electric searchlight. This is 180 ft above the sea. The way up to the crow's-nest is by iron steps within the hollow steel mast. The door leading to this is on the fifth deck below.

"Atlantic ships and some vessels of other lines have swimming baths, racquet courts, gymnasia and Turkish baths.

"On these giant ships there are also electric lifts for passengers, moving up and down five decks, and shops, a greenhouse for hothouse plants, with a gardener to look after the plants on board. There is a telephone system and exchange for 900 telephones. Worldwide news received by Marconi wireless is printed in the *Daily Mail Atlantic* of Cunard ships, and other lines have their own Press. Printing goes on at night, and passengers have papers at breakfast-time.

"The Ark, according to information we have in the Bible, must have been a vessel of some 15,000 tons. Our floating palaces of to-day are 50,000 ton ships, which can carry 4,000 or 5,000 souls in comfort as well as many thousand tons of cargo. With engines of some 100,000 horse power they plough their way through the dark blue ocean at a speed of nearly 30 miles an hour, leaving a wash for miles astern."

This quote from the 1926 book *The Largest Ships in the World* conveys some of the awe in which the great liners of the era were held. The kudos of the Blue Riband prize, an award for the fastest crossing of the Atlantic, ensured that these huge boats were an investment in national pride and honor, as well as the most vivid demonstration of the power of the new technology that was sweeping the globe. In their time they were the biggest man-made objects that could move— and they moved powerfully fast, breaking all the previous speed records and journey times. As the equivalent size of various small towns plying the

oceans, the great liners were built to be enjoyed, savored and lived in for their style and their luxury. Although the glory days of the great liners have now passed, their successors still survive and ply their trade across the waves.

The historical definition of an ocean liner was an ocean-traversing passenger vessel that ran over a fixed route and on a fixed schedule. The liner originally had three basic variants (though many different classes evolved to fill different roles): the superliner, the express liner, and the passenger-cargo liner. Nowadays their descendents are the cruise ships that ply the seas filled with holidaymakers seeking fun and luxury.

Superliners once sailed between Western Europe and the United States, and represented the ultimate

RIGHT: A cross sectional diagram through the girth of a Cunard liner from the company's heyday, revealing the functions of different areas of the vessel and its sheer scale.

development of the liner form. These vessels had a gross registered tonnage (GRT) that eventually exceeded 50,000 tons. They offered the most luxurious passenger accommodation as well as cheaper, less glamorous "steerage," with room for about 2,500-3,000 passengers. Their speed also increased with their size, up to about 30 knots (in fact the USS *United States* managed over 35 knots). The names of the great superliners were known throughout the world as bywords for speed, power, and luxury.

Express liner existed where mail and express cargo called for a fast worldwide shipping service. With a GRT of between 20–30,000, the passenger accommodation totaled approximately 1,500 and the speed was up to 25 knots. They were somewhat smaller than their huge Atlantic cousins by virtue of the various canals through which they had to pass en route and the smaller ports that they had to enter.

Another category was the passenger-cargo combination liner, which generally operated on routes where cargo, rather than passengers or mail, was the main consideration. Such services were worldwide, and the average ship had a GRT of up to 25,000, room for around 8-10,000 tons of general cargo, and accommodation for up to 500 passengers.

The modern cruise ship, a descendent of the superliner, is no longer designed for the mass transportation of people; this is a role carried out by the airline industry. Instead they exist as floating hotels, visiting tourist and holiday hotspots around the world. These vessels are still luxuriously appointed, though not quite to the extent of the superliners. With transatlantic passenger

RIGHT: Another of Cunard's posters from the golden age of liners. The company was the first ever to offer a regularly scheduled transatlantic passenger service on *Britannia* from 1840.

BELOW: Cunard is still in business today after over a century and a half of operating passenger services. This is the *Cunard Countess* at Castries Harbour in St. Lucia. The vessel has recently been sold to Awani Cruises of Indonesia for £18 million.

ABOVE: The enormous bulk of the steamship *Great Eastern* rises above a knot of workers helping to launch her. It took over two months and six tries to launch the ship. Although the vessel, considered the prototype of the modern ocean liners, could carry 4,000 passengers in addition to her crew, she was never successful as a passenger liner and was sold and used as a cable vessel.

trade now wholly dominated by the airlines, these ships service the higher end of the tourist trade, fulfilling the carefully planned itineraries of pleasure cruises.

In their time the great ocean liners revolutionized sea transportation, and up until the 1960s were the only way to convey large amounts of people and cargo to other continents. The complete domination of the airline industry today hides the fact that the liner was the only form of transport available. For some these journeys may have been the epitome of pleasure, but the vast majority of journeys made and passengers carried were more prosaic in character. The only realistic and reliable form of mass transportation, the liners

transported all the waves of mass migration that characterized the late 19th and early 20th centuries.

Like the commercial airline battles today the shipping lines fought desperately for the business, their rivalry fuelled not only by commercial considerations but also by national pride. Driven forward by these intense pressures, many of the great ships were built at a loss, subsidized by governments desperate to see them succeed. These same considerations led to the blossoming of the liner into its golden period in the middle years of the 20th century, just before it was overtaken by a form of transportation whose development was accelerated by the World War II—mass air transportation, as obsolete bombers were converted into the first mail, cargo, and passenger carriers. Though other large vessels have been constructed, such as aircraft carriers and bulk carriers, none have the same level of luxurious complexity or romantic magic of the liners. Indeed, the largest ships today, bulk carriers and container ships, are simply

mammoth, nigh on featureless, floating storage containers filled with oil, grain, sand, coal, or cement, a strictly functional approach to transporting cargo.

Some of the companies that service the modern cruise and ferry market are the same as those that prospered during the golden age of the liner. Two names in particular bear special mention—P&O and Cunard. These two dominated the superliner market through much of the period. Cunard concentrated on the Atlantic routes, eventually taking over the White Star Line while P&O performed a complex schedule of routes to India, the Far East, and Australia, eventually taking over the Orient Line. Cunard's fleet totaled some 250, whilst P&O were the largest with 450 vessels over the period from when they were first

inaugurated up to modern times. A healthy recognition of the market and an ability to adapt has enabled these old companies to survive the changes to the market. They have launched a new range of modern cruise ships to replace the veteran liners of the golden age, as well as streamlining their businesses, cutting costs, and taking over the competition. This newer market continues to expand and flourish, especially in the USA, with the increase in trade making the reappearance of the larger liners a possibility.

Birth of the Liner

The end of the 19th century saw the world increasingly transformed by technological change as the Industrial Revolution brought about remarkable advances. Man's mastery over the forces of nature had increased enormously with the advent of the steam engine, and this was reflected especially in the transport systems of the time. This process was particularly

BELOW: Machinery dwarfs the workers in the paddle engine room of the *Great Eastern*. The steamship boasted two screw propellers, two paddle wheels, and a battery of sails on six masts.

dramatic in the field of seaborne transport as the age of sail gave way to the age of steam. The beautiful hand-crafted wooden sailing ships, driven by a complicated system of sails and rigging, gave way to steam-pow-ered, riveted, iron-hulled vessels that could cross oceans in a fraction of the time it had taken their pre-decessors. A number of experimental steam-powered ships were built in the late 18th century. In the USA in 1807, Robert Fulton's *Clermont* made the 150 mile (240 km) trip from New York City to Albany in 32 hours. Also *Savannah*, a fully-rigged US sailing ship 99 ft long with a GRT of 320 was specially fitted with engines and paddlewheels and made the first Atlantic crossing by a steam-propelled vessel in 1819, though her sails were used as well. These developments enabled the manufacturers to create vessels that had a vastly increased capacity in terms of both volume of cargo and passenger numbers. The late 19th century was also a period of great growth in the world econo-my and trade, along with a huge increase in population and migration, creating a market for these vessels and spurring their development onto greater heights.

As with many of the events of the Industrial Revolution, Britain was at the forefront of this whirl-wind of change. She had a history of shipbuilding and naval prowess due to her location and overseas empire, and was the first to revolutionize her industry with the new techniques. In 1828, *Great Western* was built by Isambard Kingdom Brunel especially for the Atlantic run and in 1838 *Sirius*, another British steamship crossed in a journey time of 16 and a half days. In 1840, the of Cunard's passenger vessel, the SS *Britannia*, a wooden paddle steamer 207 ft long and 1,1154 GRT was the first ship to cross the Atlantic entirely under steam power and take the Blue Riband. The Cunard Line was founded by Samuel Cunard in 1840, using four small, wooden steam-paddle driven ships named *Britannia*, *Acadia* (also a Blue Riband holder), *Caledonia,* and *Columbia*. The aim was to provide a regularly scheduled steam mail service across the Atlantic, offering weekly departures. This

powered by eight engines, divided between screws and paddles, and she also bore the hallmark of modern ship design in that she was double skinned and therefore a ship within a ship, with watertight compartmentation. She was built for the Australian and Eastern routes, designed to hold enough coal for the entire journey. However, passengers did not like her exaggerated roll and she ended up being sold. Her late claim to fame was in laying the first Atlantic cables between the USA and the UK. Being such a revolutionary ship there were many problems in her construction and launch and Brunel never saw her sail: he died shortly before her launch, worn out by this innovative and difficult project.

It was 41 years before any ship surpassed the *Great Eastern* in length and that vessel was the *Oceanic*. Built in 1899 by Harland & Wolff in Belfast for the White Star Company, she was the first steel ship and was 705 ft long. She was narrower than the *Great Eastern* with several other design changes, notably the flat floor and sharp turn of the double-plated bilge, which made her almost a rectangle in shape.

The Boom in Business

By this time other European countries had joined in the steamship race and the competition soon increased dramatically with the rise in trade and mass migration. In fact, the commercial intensity led to the eruption of a corporate war as the various lines of Britain, France, Germany, and eventually, America, all seeking the lion's share of the transatlantic passenger trade, constantly tried to outdo each other with the largest, fastest, and most luxurious vessels ever built.

The transatlantic route was the finest liner route in terms of profitability and prestige, and therefore attracted the largest vessels. Whilst the Peninsular and Oriental Company, P&O, had the largest fleet it had no particularly large vessels. The nature of their different trade routes placed a limit on the class and size of ships required, in particular, the opening of the Suez Canal 1869 limited the size of vessels traveling on the route to India to below 30,000 GRT. The opening of the Panama Canal in 1915 had a similar effect on size and GRT of liners.

But from now on the builders of the Atlantic liners forced the pace in big-ship building, as each nation

was a huge improvement over the sailing packets of the day, which sailed regular schedules but suffered the vagaries of the weather. It provided the impetus for Great Britain to dominate the Atlantic trade, since the US was slow to take up steam as a means of ocean crossing—though steamships were already in use on river and inland waters.

Cunard's first ships could cross the Atlantic in just over 11 days and they began what was to become over 100 years of leadership and constant competition to all others who tried to operate a service between the continents. Others were doing the same, including the British Great Western Company, which made the wooden paddle steamer *Great Britain* in 1843. The first all-iron steamship was Cunard's 3,300 GRT *Persia*, built in 1856 and winner of the Blue Riband in a time of just over nine days. She was followed by the *Great Eastern*, a paddle and screw steamer again built by the redoubtable Isambard Kingdom Brunel in 1858. At 18,914 GRT she was 692 ft long, twice the size of the *Persia*. She had six masts, five of iron and one of wood, enough for some 7,000 yards of sail, she was

sought to have the largest and most impressive ship in the world. Within 14 years of the launch of the *Oceanic*, tonnage and length increased exponentially and some ports were soon too shallow to berth these huge ships. The competition intensified at the turn of the 20th century, when the newly formed German nation started to develop an international-caliber fleet. Their aims were twofold; to divert the economic benefits derived from mastery of the transatlantic routes away from Great Britain, and also to win the Blue Riband prize, thus bolstering national pride and identity. In 1897, this second goal was achieved by their impressive new flagship, the North German-Lloyd Line's 655 ft, 14,349 GRT *Kaiser Wilhelm der Grosse*. She was not only faster than the leading British ships, but also larger and more luxuriously appointed as well, and was only the first in a fleet of still larger and faster ships planned. In 1900, another German shipping line,

Hamburg-Amerika, set a new Atlantic speed record with their new 16,500 GRT *Deutschland*.

Meanwhile, in 1901, competition of a different kind began in the USA, when the railroad magnate and financier John Pierpont Morgan, formed the International Mercantile Marine with the sole intention of monopolizing the Atlantic liner trade. He then took over numerous European companies such as the White Star Line and Red Star Line and even made an attempt to take-over Cunard. This aroused a certain amount of concern in Great Britain, as in case of war

BELOW RIGHT: The record-breaking German ship, *Kaiser Wilhelm der Grosse*, sitting in harbor at New York.

BELOW: Passengers relax onboard an ocean liner during the "golden age" before air travel. Ocean voyages, for the wealthy at least, were elegant and comfortable social occasions.

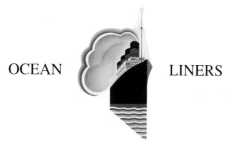

Britain's merchant fleet was an important part of her national strategy. Cunard's management took advantage of this national feeling, which when combined with clever use of political influence enabled them to secure a twenty-year low-interest loan of £2,600,000, to build two of the largest and fastest ships in the world at that time. In return, the company guaranteed to remain British-owned, and their ships were also designed for use in war with their decks and bulkheads reinforced.

A direct result of this was that the *Mauretania* was built on Tyneside by Swan, Hunter, and Richardson, while the *Lusitania* was constructed by John Brown and Co. of Clydebank, Scotland. Both companies were encouraged to experiment with their basic designs. *Mauretania* at 790 ft and 31,983 GRT was slightly larger and longer than her sister, the *Lusitania*, whose proportions were 785 ft and 31,550 GRT. Although the

two sister ships closely resembled each other externally, small differences in deck accoutrements gave the *Lusitania* cleaner lines. More importantly, the ships featured steam turbine propulsion (and different kinds of propeller—*Lusitiania* having less effective three-bladed props, whilst *Mauretania* had more efficient four-bladed ones). *Lusitania* was the first to be launched, in June 1906, but during her trials a vibration problem was discovered and she was returned to her builders for extensive interior modifications. This helped improve things to a degree, but the problem remained for the rest her short career. *Mauretania* would also have a problem with vibration, but never as severe as *Lusitania*—which took several crossings before she won the Blue Riband from her German rivals in 1907 . In the process she became the first ship ever to cross the Atlantic in less than five days. *Mauretania* made her maiden voyage on November

16, 1907, and immediately proved herself to be a very fast ship, though it took her a number of trips before she snatched the Blue Riband from the *Lusitania*. Both ships continued to beat the other's records until the *Mauretania* turned in her best pre-war performance of 26.25 knots, a record she kept for over 20 years. These impressive and reliable ships were also more luxuriously appointed than any that had come before, each featuring a strikingly different interior. Yet although they were making huge profits for Cunard, the company deemed it necessary to have another big ship so as to be able to guarantee weekly sailings from both sides of the Atlantic. So the 45,600 GRT *Aquitania* entered service in June 1914, only two months before the outbreak of World War I. Considerably larger than her older sisters, unlike them she was not built for speed but followed the latest Atlantic trend for vessels that were slower, stabler, and more luxuriously appointed, such as White Star's *Olympic* and the Hamburg-

Amerika's *Imperator*. *Aquitania* would go on to provide Cunard with over 35 years of reliable service and would also serve Great Britain in both World Wars.

The White Star Line was the only serious British Atlantic competitor to Cunard, having enjoyed financial success in the last decades of the 19th century with a fleet of ships of growing size. After their US takeover they sought to counter the success of Cunard's *Mauretania* and *Lusitania*, by launching a daring plan to build three huge vessels to outdo their rivals. They followed the trend for size, stability, and comfort rather than speed. Constructed side-by-side in gantries specially built by Harland & Wolff in Belfast, the 45,000 GRT *Olympic* was first completed and launched on October 20, 1910, making her maiden voyage on June 14, 1911. The ill-fated 45,000 GRT, 883 ft *Titanic* had been launched on May 31, a fortnight before, beginning her maiden voyage on April 10, 1912—one of the most well documented and

disastrous voyages in history. The *Titanic* struck an iceberg, slicing a great hole in her side. Within two hours, six of the ship's watertight compartments had flooded causing the great ship to break in two and sink. Over 1,500 people lost their lives due principally to a fatal lack of lifeboats.

The lasting upside of the *Titanic* disaster was the immediate improvement of safety at sea, with new laws passed requiring a lifeboat place for all onboard any ship. The White Star Line would never really recover from this disaster, though both *Olympic* and *Britannic* underwent costly refits to give them new

BELOW LEFT: The Blue Riband winning *Mauretania* undergoing repairs in Newcastle, UK.

BELOW: The luxurious British Cunard ocean liner *Lusitania*, in the early 1900s. She was destroyed by a German submarine's torpedo on May 7, 1915, an act which increased the pressure on the American government to intervene militarily against Germany.

double-skinned, longitudinal bulkheads and more lifeboats. The third ship, *Britannic*, was the largest of the three sisters at 50,000 GRT, launched on February 26, 1914, she would, however, never see civilian use. Instead, she was hurriedly converted to become a hospital ship and on her maiden voyage, December 23, 1915, sailed for the Mediterranean where she served in the Dardanelles Campaign alongside her sister ship *Olympic*. On November 21, 1916, she struck a mine and sank. After the war the White Star Line received the uncompleted German liner, *Bismarck*, as compensation and she was renamed *Majestic*, one of the traditional fleet names.

Meanwhile, having realized that speed in itself didn't necessarily guarantee profits Germany now set about constructing some of the largest and most luxurious ships seen for almost 20 years. In 1912, Kaiser Wilhelm II launched the 52,117 GRT *Imperator*, a veritable floating palace decorated with

The Cunard Liner
LUSITANIA

vast quantities of marble and gilt. The exterior of the ship was criticized for looking top-heavy (not helped by the monstrous 30 ft bronze Imperial eagle mounted on the bow). This top-heaviness had the unfortunate effect of causing the vessel to roll even in the calmest seas, something that was not popular with passengers.

The Effects of War and Beyond

In 1914, the 54,117 GRT *Vaterland* began Atlantic service for the Hamburg-Amerika Line. She was even more luxuriously appointed than her consort *Imperator*. Her public rooms contained a design first;

LEFT: A White Star Line poster advertising *Olympic* and *Titanic*.

BELOW: The ocean liner, *S.S. Imperator*, heads out of Upper New York Bay to the Atlantic Ocean. ca. 1913, New York.

the funnel uptakes were routed along the side of the ship, thus allowing much more space in the interior of the vessel. The Kaiser himself launched the last of the German trio of superliners, the 56,551 GRT *Bismarck*, in 1914, but she did not see Atlantic service, as World War I intervened. *Kaiser Wilhelm II*, *Kronprinz Wilhelm*, and *Vaterland*, would all be tied up in American ports at the outbreak of war and would eventually be taken over by the USA for use as "troopers"—ships used to carry the troops to France. The enormous *Vaterland* was renamed *Leviathan*.

The outbreak of war would also cut short Cunard's dream of a tri-weekly service; *Aquitania* and *Mauretania* were both requisitioned for war duties, while *Lusitania* remained briefly in her civilian role on the Atlantic run. *Mauretania* and *Aquitania* would quickly prove themselves too under-armored and coal-hungry to act as auxiliary cruisers, so instead they

served as troopers and hospital ships. On May 7, 1915, *Lusitania* was torpedoed by a German submarine and sank in less than 20 minutes, before many of the lifeboats could be successfully launched. This caused the loss of over 1,195 lives.

After the war, Cunard received the German liner *Imperator* as compensation and renamed her *Berengaria*. For the next 15 years Cunard operated the three biggest liners, *Mauretaina*, *Aquitania,* and *Berengaria*, while rebuilding the rest of the fleet with more modestly sized vessels. Though there were plans for other superliners these were put on hold, for the world had not yet recovered from the economic depression, and shipping lines were particularly hard hit when the United States started imposing immigration controls.

In 1922, following a German postwar recovery, North German Lloyd launched the 32,300 GRT *Columbus*. She would be the company's new flagship until in the late 1920s it boldly announced plans to construct two huge high-speed liners, *Bremen* and *Europa*. These two ships were launched on successive days in August 1928. Both these vessels had radical new designs, including two squat, streamlined funnels, rounded sterns for increased speed and efficiency, and below the waterline they had bulbous bows that greatly reduced water drag. *Europa* was originally planned to launch first; however, she was nearly destroyed in a serious fire at her Hamburg docks, which delayed completion for another year. *Bremen* was delivered on schedule and immediately proved herself in terms of speed. In 1929, she shattered the record held by *Mauretania*, creating a new average record speed of

RIGHT: A poster advertising the cruising services of the German Hamburg-Amerika line, a powerful force in the North Atlantic passenger business.

BELOW: The doomed *Titanic* sets out on her maiden voyage.

27.83 knots. In 1930, *Europa* too would win the Blue Riband, but lost out to the *Bremen* soon afterward. After this Germany lost the Blue Riband for good, first to the Italians, then the French and the British. They never again mounted another successful Blue Riband challenge. *Bremen*'s fate was to be destroyed by fire during the war, and after the war Germany's one remaining superliner, *Europa*, was given to France as part of their war reparations. Germany would never build an Atlantic superliner again.

After World War I the USA converted the *Leviathan* from a trooper back to a superliner and ran her on the North Atlantic run, but she was never able to achieve a profit, often sailing only half full. This was partly due to immigration controls but also Prohibition, for American ships were "dry" alcohol-free vessels, while their competitors were not. The United States Line then introduced the smaller and more profitable liners *Manhattan* and *Washington*, both at around 24,000 GRT. The largest ship built for America before World War II was the 34,000 GRT *America*, launched in 1939.

The French Line, Compagnie Generale Transatlantique, also did not enter the Atlantic superliner competition until after World War I. Earlier they had operated a collection of smaller but fashionable liners, the largest and most famous of which was *France*, 23,769 GRT and 713 ft long, and famous for its sumptuously modeled interiors. *Paris* was one of the first new large liners commissioned after the war and at 34,500 GRT she was the French Line's largest ship to date, her lavish state rooms became a byword for transatlantic luxury.

Italy also did not enter the transatlantic superliner trade until after World War I. In 1926, the Navigazione Generale Italiana (NGI), with the help of Mussolini's fascist government, launched the largest diesel-powered liner ever built at the time—the 30,400 GRT *Augustus*. By the end of the 1930s the three largest Italian lines had all merged to become the huge Italia Line, which was again encouraged by Mussolini in their efforts to build a new Atlantic superliner in the hope of capturing the Blue Riband for Italy. The NGI

had already begun construction of the 51,000 GRT *Rex* while the Lloyd Sabaudo was doing much the same with the 48,500 GRT *Conte di Savoia*. These two new liners would enter into service just two months apart in 1932 and both would suffer problems on their maiden voyages. The *Rex* eventually proved herself by taking the Blue Riband in August 1933, with a time of four days, 13 hours. Both superliners were destroyed in the war.

In 1927, the French Line commissioned one of the most famous liners ever built, *Ile de France*. She would become renowned, not for her size (791 ft, 43,153 GRT) or technological sophistication, but for the bold and fresh style of her revolutionary new art deco interiors. By 1935 she was carrying more first-class travelers than any other liner. Next, despite the bleak economic depression of the period, the French government helped to subsidize the cost of one

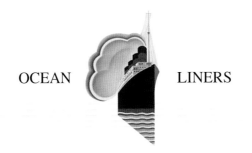

the largest liners ever built, *Normandie*, at a cost of over $60,000,000. Launched on October 29, 1932, she was the first ship to exceed 70,000 GRT and to be over 1,000 ft in length. Like *Ile de France*, the *Normandie*'s interiors were extraordinarily luxurious and her clean, sleek external features, both above and below the waterline, influenced ocean liner design for decades. To the joy of the French, *Normandie* won the Blue Riband prize on her maiden voyage on May 29, 1935. She covered the distance in four days, three hours, and two minutes, averaging just under 30 knots for the whole crossing.

LEFT: The S.S. *Washington* heads up the Hudson past Manhattan on April 30, 1933.

BELOW LEFT: A painting of *America*—the largest vessel in the US before World War II.

BELOW: Tugboats help to guide the *Queen Mary* into the 51st Street Pier as she arrives in New York City in 1936.

In Great Britain, Cunard had began work on the superliner *Queen Mary* in 1932, however, financial problems caused the project to grind to a halt. In 1934 the British government forced the merger of the White Star and Cunard Lines and this enabled the work to restart. The 81,235 GRT, 1,019 ft *Queen Mary* was launched the same year, in September 1934. She was traditional in appearance, resembling the liners of earlier years more than the sleeker modern European ships; however, she was a fast ship, winning the Blue Riband from her French rival *Normandie* in August 1936. The prize would then pass between the two ships until August 1938 when the *Queen Mary* crossed the Atlantic in three days, 20 hours, and 40 minutes. She held this record for over 20 years. The *Queen Mary* was also to prove much more economically successful than the *Normandie*, which routinely traveled only 60 percent full. The outbreak of World War II cut short the commercial careers of these two giant

liners. Initially they languished in New York where they were joined by the hastily completed *Queen Elizabeth* in March 1940, which had sailed secretly to America to prevent her becoming an enemy target. Both *Queen Mary* and *Queen Elizabeth* then sailed to Australia to be converted into troopers, whereas *Normandie* came to a tragic end. After being renamed the USS *Lafayette* and while being converted to a trooper she caught fire and eventually capsized having become top-heavy through the vast quantities of water pumped into her. Though salvaged she was discovered to be too badly damaged and scrapped.

The post-War Years

After the war, the Cunard Line found that they had the Atlantic market cornered, *Queen Mary* and *Queen Elizabeth* were two of the few survivors among the great pre-war liners. Only the ex-German liner *Europa*, now ceded to the French, was around to provide a worthy rival. During the 1950s, the *Queen Mary* and *Queen Elizabeth* provided Cunard

with record profits and maintained the reputation of the line.

Italy launched two large ships in 1954, *Cristoforo Columbo* and *Andrea Doria*. *Andrea Doria* was subsequently lost in a collision in fog with the Swedish liner *Stockholm* on July 25, 1956. In 1960, the Italia Line launched an even larger ship, *Leonardo da Vinci*, which was 33,000 GRT. Later in 1965 Italy made the most of the short lived European sea travel revival, with the building of two 45,000 GRT sister ships, *Michelangelo* and *Raffaello*. Though initially popular they were both taken out of service in the early 1970s when the passenger liner trade collapsed.

In 1962 the French Line would replace the *Europa*, renamed *Liberté*, with a new ship, *France*. Initially she proved popular on the Atlantic route, with her renowned French cuisine and distinctive winged funnels. However, in 1974 the French government withdrew its subsidy and *France* was retired.

PREVIOUS PAGE: The Russian liner *Fedor Dostoevsky* **in Scotland.**

LEFT: The *Washington* **leaves Brooklyn Army Base on her maiden voyage as a US army transport with approximately 3,000 troops, bound for Panama, Philipine Islands, and Hawai.**

BELOW: A rescue helicopter hovers over the Swedish ship *Stockholm***, about 45 miles south of Nantucket Island, July 26, 1956, as it prepares to pick up injured survivors for transfer to the Nantucket Hospital. The** *Stockholm* **later slowly made her way to New York with 533 survivors from sunken** *Andrea Doria***.**

The American government, having witnessed the success of using *Queen Mary* and *Queen Elizabeth* as troopers during the war, voted a $48 million dollar subsidy to finance their own large high-speed Atlantic liner, the 50,000 GRT *United States*. She was a technological sensation and the fastest ship ever produced, the first fireproof ship and convertible to a trooper in a matter of days. On her maiden voyage in July 1952, the *United States* set a new record for the Blue Riband prize, averaging 35.59 knots and cutting ten hours from the *Queen Mary*'s best time. *United States* and *America* operated together until 1965, when falling trade forced the sale of *America*. Four years later in 1969 the US government withdrew its subsidy and the *United States* was retired.

During 1960s and 70s the growth of cheap air travel proved to be the death knell of the great passenger liners, whose trade diminished until they were almost all retired. The *Queen Mary* became a floating museum and hotel at Long Beach, California. Her sister ship, the *Queen Elizabeth*, was sold to the Far East and destroyed by accidental fire in 1972.

In 1967, Cunard's next flagship, the 68,863 GRT 963 ft *Queen Elizabeth 2* was launched, making her maiden voyage in 1969. The *QE2* continues to make occasional transatlantic crossings but mainly functions as a cruise ship.

However, despite coming close to extinction, the passenger ships are once again coming back in the guise of cruise ships. No longer used for any schedule other than cruising, they are have been increasing in numbers and size.

PREVIOUS PAGE: The modern Russian passenger liner *Kladjya Yelansjya.*

LEFT: Bridge of the *United States.* The ship's telegraph is used to transmit the captain's orders to the engine room.

BELOW: A view of the liner *Leonardo da Vinci,* launched by the Italia Line in 1960.

RIGHT & BELOW RIGHT: Thomson Holiday's *Topaz* is typical of the older-style of cruise vessel; up to 1,050 passengers can enjoy the swimming pool and whirlpool, two restaurants, four bars, two lounges, discotheque, shopping arcade, children's playroom, and gym. the ship also has business facilities.

OCEAN LINERS

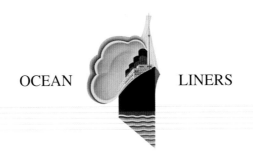

ABOVE: The *Royal Viking Queen* liner typifies today's perfectly appointed cruise liners.

LEFT: *Royal Viking Sky*, pictured in 1989, prepares to sail from Leith Docks in Edinburgh.

ABOVE RIGHT: *Sea Princess*, owned by Princess Cruises and launched in 1998, docked at Ocho Rios, Jamaica.

RIGHT: *Seabourn Pride*, operated by Seabourn Cruises Inc., was launched in 1988.

T

HE LINERS

The Liners

Explanatory Notes

Within this A-Z list of ocean liners old and new, each vessel has been headed with preliminary information in the following standardized format as follows. This is followed by an appraisal of each vessel, or class, giving its history and details of what kind of amenities the traveler would expect to find onboard.

Name and Years of Active Service

Owner—Former names and year of name change.

Type—Description of status and passenger capacity.

Builders—Yard number and date launched or floated, where known.

Dimensions—Gross Registered Tonnage; overall length in feet and meters; overall beam in feet and meters.

Machinery—Type of main propulsion; number of screw propellers or propulsion units.

PREVIOUS PAGES: P&O's Oriana, launched in 1995, and boasting 914 cabins, a four-story waterfall, and a four star superior rating caused something of a stir when she was hit by a freak wave in the Atlantic in 1999 while en route for Southampton, UK. Luckily, none of the passengers or crew were seriously hurt.

Gross Registered Tonnage

To enable the reader to compare like with like in terms of size, a more detailed explanation of the term Gross Registered Tonnage (GRT) is in order. One might reasonably conclude that the larger the tonnage (GRT), the larger, visually, the ship. However, this is not necessarily true as Gross Registered Tonnage is fundamentally the measure of the direct revenue-earning cubic space (one hundred cubic feet equaling one ton) within a ship. Thus, it is heavily influenced by how the space available for this purpose is utilized.

The characteristics of the old route passenger liners, with their much larger power plants and fine hull forms for high service speeds, were unlike those of modern cruise ships which, to fulfil a quite different function, have towering superstructures constructed over relatively shallow and quite flat-bottomed hulls. As a consequence, the space utilization within the hull dimensions of passenger vessels conceived for these contrasting roles can give tonnage figures dramatically at variance with their actual proportions or, conversely, the ships can appear to be smaller than they, in fact, are.

Ideally, in order to make a more accurate comparison of size, a volumetric measure relating to the actual scale or proportions of each ship would be desirable. Such a unit of measure does not exist, however, so, in order to illustrate the point with the following examples, the principal dimensions of each has been compiled in a table to permit close comparison. The four ships that have been selected for the purposes of this comparison are all, in some way, record-breaking ships, two of them route passenger liners and two of them modern purpose-built cruise ships. A crude, volumetric capacity based on these dimensions could be calculated as a further means of conveying true size but, as a block volume, it would make no provision for hull and superstructure shape, either full or fine:

Principal Dimensions
Name: *Queen Elizabeth* (1940)—the largest passenger liner ever built
GRT: 83,675
LOA: 1,031.0 ft/314.3 m
BOA: 118.4 ft/36.1 m

Name: *Voyager of the Seas* (1999)—with two sisters, one of the largest three cruise ships so far built
GRT: 139,296
LOA: 1,020.0 ft/311.0 m
BOA: 127.9 ft/39.0 m

Name: *United States* (1952)—the fastest passenger liner ever built
GRT: 53,329
LOA: 990.0 ft/301.8 m
BOA: 101.7 ft/31.0 m
Extreme Depth: 122.0 ft/37.2 m

Name: *Carnival Destiny* (1996)—first passenger vessel to exceed 100,000 GRT
GRT: 101,353
LOA: 892.8 ft/272.2 m
BOA: 118.1 ft/36.0 m

Whereas in order of GRT alone, these four ships would probably be ranked in the order: *Voyager of the Seas, Carnival Destiny, Queen Elizabeth, United States*, in terms of the total volume calculated by their principle dimensions, they would be ranked: *Voyager of the Seas, Queen Elizabeth, United States, Carnival Destiny.*

Main Propulsion
According to their age and the nature of the role for which they were conceived, passenger ships have had a wide variety of types of main propulsion machinery installed within them, as follows:

Steam reciprocating—essentially piston-engined drive through crankshafts.
Steam turbines—both direct acting and geared.
Turbo-electric—combined steam turbines with electric drive motors.
Diesel—internal combustion drive through crankshafts, both direct acting and geared.
Diesel-electric—combined diesel with electric drive motors.
Gas turbine electric—combined gas turbines with electric drive motors.

Passenger Space Ratio
Within the passages describing individual cruise ships or classes of cruise ship, reference has been made to Passenger Space Ratios. This is a rather approximate industry measure, calculated by dividing the space dedicated to passenger use by the number of passengers carried to give a comparison of space allocation. It should be borne in mind that the actual allocation of space varies according to occupancy level. The Passenger Space Ratio figures quoted here have been based upon only one given level of occupancy and may not fully reflect the spaciousness actually experienced. Furthermore, the Passenger Space Ratio makes no distinction between cabin size and the area of public spaces. Some passengers may prefer more private space while for others the size and ambience of the public amenities, the lounges and restaurants etc., is more important.

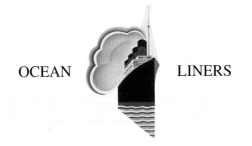
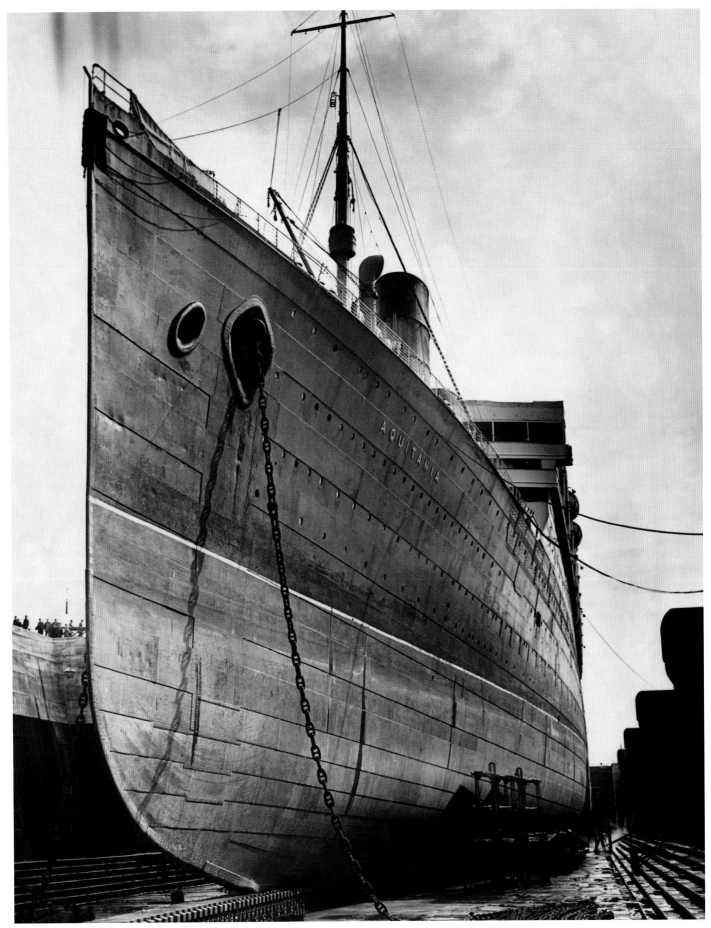

Aida (1996-)

Owner: Aida Cruises
Type: Active cruise ship—1,186 berths
Builder: Kvaerner Masa, Turku—Yard No. 1337
Dimensions: 38,531 GRT; 633 ft/193.0 m LOA; 92 ft/28.0 m BOA
Machinery: Diesel, twin screw

When she entered service, the *Aida* was the largest cruise ship under the German flag. She was a striking ship with huge eye and mouth emblems painted on her sides and around her bow, at least that is how they were described.

The *Aida* was named in a ceremony, conducted at Rostock on June 7, 1996, following the recent practice of christening vessels at a date other than that of their launch or flotation. Her original owners were Deutsche Seereederei Touristik. Following the naming ceremony, *Aida* undertook a short presentation cruise to the German ports of Kiel, Hamburg, and Bremerhaven, no doubt looking to attract local patronage for her forthcoming cruise operations. The ship's maiden cruise was to Palma de Mallorca from Bremerhaven. A regular itinerary of Mediterranean cruises followed.

Ownership of the *Aida* passed to Norwegian Cruise Line in 1997, though she was immediately leased back to her former owners. She was sold again, more recently, to Aida Cruises, a subsidiary of P&O in which Arkona Touristik holds a 49 percent stake. Two similar but slightly larger as yet unnamed ships have been ordered from the Aker MV shipyard to join the *Aida* in 2002 and 2003.

LEFT: An ocean giant in the dock, 1939. The *Aquitania* makes an impressive picture in dry dock at Southampton for overhaul and a general re-paint.

Amsterdam
see the *Rotterdam*-class

Aquitania (1914-1950)

Owner: Cunard Line
Type: Former passenger liner—3,230, later reduced to 2,200, passengers in three classes
Builder: John Brown, Clydebank—Yard No. 409, launched April 21, 1913
Dimensions: 45,645 GRT; 901 ft/274.7 m LOA; 97 ft/29.6 m BOA
Machinery: Steam turbines, quadruple screw

Epitomizing the elegance of the Edwardian era, the stately four-funneled *Aquitania* gave her owners a quarter of a century of excellent service on the North Atlantic run, besides being employed twice on auxiliary duties for her country. In fact, she had barely entered service in 1914, operating from Liverpool, when she was called-up for the first time to serve as an armed merchant cruiser—briefly—as a hospital ship, and finally as a troopship.

The *Aquitania* was returned to her owners in 1919 and immediately resumed the transatlantic scheduled service out of Southampton, interrupted only by a thorough overhaul, which included conversion from coal to oil fuel. For the next 20 years she maintained regular sailings between Southampton and New York alongside the larger *Berengaria* and the celebrated *Mauretania*, then still the holder of the Atlantic Blue Riband. All three were units of the famous inter-war "Big Six" group of Atlantic passenger liners.

In September 1939, the *Aquitania* was once more requisitioned for war service, utilized throughout as a troopship. Over the six years of her military engagement she steamed more than half a million miles and transported almost 339,000 servicemen to and from the war zones.

By the time she was returned to Cunard for the second time she was completely exhausted and deemed to be unworthy of a full restoration. She had, in fact, survived her planned retirement by six years for Cunard's intention had been to replace her in 1940 with the *Queen Elizabeth*. Despite this, the *Aquitania* continued in operation for another two years, working an austere emigrant service to Halifax, Nova Scotia, on behalf of the Canadian Government. Her long career finally ended in February 1950 when she was paid off to be broken up at Faslane, Scotland.

Arcadia (1989-)

Owner: P&O Cruises—ex *Star Princess* (1997), ex *Sitmar Fair Majesty* (1989)
Type: Active cruise ship—1,621 berths
Builder: Chantiers et Ateliers de L'Atlantique—Yard No. B29, launched March 5, 1988
Dimensions: 63,524 GRT; 806 ft/245.6 m LOA; 105 ft/32.0 m BOA
Machinery: Diesel-electric, twin screw

When P&O absorbed the long established Sitmar Company in 1988 it experienced an immediate growth of its cruise fleet, permitting the replacement of some of its first generation ships of the "Love Boat" series that had been introduced in the early 1970s. Among the ships acquired was the *Sitmar Fair Majesty*, then building, which was renamed *Star Princess* on March 23, 1989, at a ceremony in Florida, shortly after delivery to her owners, Princess Cruises. She alternated between the American West Coast, making ten day cruises north to Alaska from San Francisco, and the Caribbean, based at Fort Lauderdale.

Meanwhile, the P&O cruise operation based in Southampton was going through a period of transition.

RIGHT: *Arcadia* cruising the Norwegian Fjords.

BELOW RIGHT: Another vessel taken over by P&O and renamed, *Victoria*, previously *Kungsholm*, has capacity for 722 passengers and 400 officers and crew.

BELOW: *Arcadia*, formerly known as the *Star Princess* and launched in 1988, has served on many routes around the world and is currently based in Southampton, UK.

OVERLEAF: *Star Princess* entering St. Thomas Harbour in the US Virgin Islands.

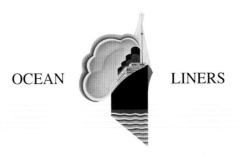

The former Swedish-flag North Atlantic liner *Kungsholm* had been taken over in 1979 and renamed *Sea Princess*. Sixteen years later, in October 1995, with the passing of the original *Oriana*, she was renamed *Victoria* to bolster the P&O Cruises operation. Recognizing that the demand for cruises out of the United Kingdom to the Mediterranean and Atlantic Islands was also growing in popularity, P&O set about building and enhancing its presence in this market. With the imminent termination of the *Canberra*'s career, two new vessels were ordered, the new *Oriana* and the *Aurora*. Between the deliveries of these two, the *Star Princess* was switched to Southampton as the *Arcadia*, reviving a popular name of a former Australia-run liner.

Aurora (2000-)

Owner: P&O Cruises
Type: Active cruise ship—1,874 berths
Builder: Meyer Werft, Papenburg—Yard No. 640, launched February 3, 1999
Dimensions: 76,152 GRT; 886 ft/270.0 m LOA; 105 ft/32.0 m BOA
Machinery: Diesel, twin screw

Second of P&O's major new cruise ships for the European branch of its operations, the *Aurora* was only the third all-new pure cruise ship constructed to the company's order since the diversification from route operations in the early 1970s. The majority of the P&O new buildings since that time had gone to Princess Cruises.

Like her earlier fleetmate, *Oriana*, the very similar though slightly larger *Aurora* experienced mechanical

ABOVE LEFT: *Aurora* **has overcome early engineering problems to become a steadfast liner, carrying passengers to the Atlantic islands and elsewhere.**

FAR LEFT: *Aurora*'s **stern, showing the distinctive poolside.**

LEFT: **The indoor Crystal Pool.**

OVERLEAF: **Larger than** *Oriana*, *Aurora* **has 1,874 berths, indicating the growing demand for luxury cruises.**

problems when she first entered service. The nature of the problem was overheating of a propeller shaft bearing, forcing the abandonment of her inaugural cruise on May 2, 2000. After disembarking her 1,800 passengers at Southampton she sailed to Hamburg for repairs by Blohm & Voss. Cancellations of subsequent cruises did not give the ship the kind of publicity that P&O had hoped for her and the sight of a brand new, super cruise ship, the focus of high profile media attention, limping back to her home port did not go down well. These difficulties have now been resolved though and the *Aurora* has settled into her program of cruises, helping to rebuild Southampton's importance as a major passenger port. Like the *Oriana* and *Arcadia*, her cruise itinerary takes her to the Mediterranean and the Atlantic islands of Madeira and the Canaries as well as further afield.

Berengaria (1913-1938)

Owner: Cunard Line—ex *Imperator* (1921)
Type: Former passenger liner—4,594, later reduced to 2,723 passengers in four classes
Builder: Bremer Vulkan, Hamburg—Yard No. 314, launched May 23, 1912
Dimensions: 52,225 GRT; 919 ft/285.7 m LOA; 98 ft/29.9 m BOA
Machinery: Steam turbines, quadruple screw

The first of three giant passenger liners planned by the huge German shipping group, the Hamburg-Amerika Line, the *Imperator* entered service in June 1913 when she made her maiden voyage from Cuxhaven to New York. Just over a year later she was laid-up at her home port for the duration of World War I.

The *Imperator* became a war reparation, allocated to the Cunard Line as compensation for the torpedoed *Lusitania* in a combined deal which saw her consort *Bismarck* taken over by White Star Line as the *Majestic*. Cunard had the *Imperator* refurbished and converted to oil burning. Renamed *Berengaria*, she re-entered the North Atlantic express passenger and

ABOVE: *Berengaria* (previously *Imperator*)—on the right—was awarded to Cunard as reparation for the torpedoed *Lusitania*. To the left is White Star Line's *Olympic*.

mail service in May 1921. Less popular than her new fleetmates, she nevertheless outlived both her younger half-sisters as an active liner.

With the entry into service of the *Queen Mary* in 1936, the *Berengaria*'s days were numbered. She survived for two more years, but an outbreak of fire at New York in March 1938 was her death knell. Refused clearance to embark passengers, she crossed the Atlantic empty for her final voyage and was then sent to the scrapyard at Jarrow.

Big Red Boat I (1965-)

Owner: Premier Cruises—ex *Starship Oceanic* (1999), ex *Royale Oceanic* (1985), ex *Oceanic* (1985)
Type: Active converted passenger liner—1,562 berths
Builder: Cantieri Riuniti dell'Adriatico—Yard `No. 1876, launched January 15, 1963
Dimensions: 39,240 GRT; 782.0 ft/238.4 m LOA; 95.1 ft/29.0 m BOA
Machinery: Steam turbines, quadruple screw

When the *Oceanic* was conceived in the early 1960s, her then owners, the Home Line, were still a major player on the emigrant services to Australia, New Zealand, and Canada. Recognizing that this trade was rapidly disappearing, the *Oceanic* was recast as a cruise ship, one of the first conversions of its type. So it was, when the *Oceanic* made her first departure on March 31, 1965, instead of entering the Cuxhaven to Montreal service, as originally intended, she crossed to New York where she was based for an annual program of cruises to the Bahamas.

This phase of the *Oceanic*'s career extended for the next 20 years, until a change of ownership in 1985 when she was renamed *Starship Oceanic*. Her new owners were Premier Cruise Line, the operating company for Cruise Holidays, for whom she continued to make cruises focussed on the American market. For a period, Carnival Corporation held a stake in the Premier Cruises operation, but with the termination of this arrangement, and when flagging fortunes hit the company in the late 1990s, the former *Oceanic* found herself the victim of a dubious rebranding exercise. Renamed *Big Red Boat I* in 1999, this graceful cruise ship's future has been left uncertain with the failure of Premier Cruises on September 14, 2000.

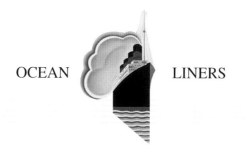

ABOVE: Holidaymakers enjoying the *Big Red Boat I*'s onboard casino. Although she has provided sterling service for nearly 40 years her future is uncertain.

The *Oceanic* was notable for having one of the first retractable "Magrodome" installations that permitted her upper lido deck area to be covered over by a retractable transparent canopy whenever inclement weather was encountered.

Big Red Boat III (1962-)

Owner: Premier Cruises—ex *Island Breeze* (2000), ex *Festivale* (1996), ex *S.A. Vaal* (1977), ex *Transvaal Castle* (1966)
Type: Active converted passenger liner—1,432 berths
Builder: John Brown, Clydebank—Yard No. 720, launched January 17, 1961
Dimensions: 38,175 GRT; 760 ft/231.7 m LOA; 89 ft/27.0 m BOA
Machinery: Steam turbines, quadruple screw

This former Union Castle mail liner has moved around a fair deal in her long career (especially in the last four to five years), a pattern of events that is typical of other aging passenger ships. She entered the scheduled Southampton to Cape Town service on January 18, 1962, switching to the associated South African company Safmarine in January 1966 along with the *Pretoria Castle*. As the *S.A. Vaal* and *S.A. Oranje*, the pair continued on the Cape run for another 11 years, the balance of their employment progressively shifting away from line voyages to cruises.

In 1977, the *S.A. Vaal* was sold to the still quite infant Carnival Corporation for conversion into the dedicated cruise ship *Festivale*. She looked striking in her new colors, enjoying a new lease of life and working out of Miami on West Indies cruises alongside the *Carnivale* and *Mardi Gras*; other converted passenger liners and the new *Tropicale* helping to establish the Carnival group as a major player in the cruise business.

This phase of her life came to an end in 1996 when she was sold for continued operation to Dolphin Cruises who renamed her *Island Breeze*, later still passing to Premier Cruises. Four years later as part of a bizarre marketing exercise associated with exploitation of the liner's distinctive hull colors, which made her and her consorts instantly recognizable, she was re-christened *Big Red Boat III*, a name which hardly

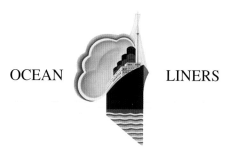
LEFT: *Tropicale*, of the Carnival Cruise Line fleet was launched in 1981 and can carry 1,796 passengers.

BELOW LEFT: Actress Marlene Dietrich arrives in New York aboard *Bremen* in 1930.

Dimensions: 51,731 GRT; 939 ft/286.3 m LOA; 102 ft/31.1 m BOA

Machinery: Steam turbines, quadruple screw

flatters this once elegant ship. Besides this, it did nothing to help Premier Line's declining fortunes and termination of their operations from September 2000 has left the former *Transvaal Castle* with equally gloomy future prospects.

Bremen (1929-1941)

Owner: Norddeutscher Lloyd

Type: Former passenger liner—2,200 passengers in four classes

Builder: Deschimag AG Weser, Bremen—Yard No. 872, launched August 16, 1928

The *Bremen*, along with her sister-ship *Europa*, represented the resurgence of the German passenger services across the Atlantic following the setbacks of World War I. The pair also marked a major turning point in passenger liner design. Their squat funnels, long low lines and rounded cruiser sterns were a radical departure from the tall masts and funnels and the counter sterns of the previous generation of Atlantic liners. They introduced the bulbous bow, a hydrodynamic innovation extensively used since on vessels of all types as a mechanism for reducing underwater hull resistance.

BELOW: *Bremen*'s sister-ship *Europa* shared her novel design features.

The *Bremen* wrested the Atlantic Blue Riband from the *Mauretania* on her first voyage, in July 1929, with speeds of 27.83 knots westbound and 27.92 knots eastbound, thus ending the British ship's long reign as Atlantic speed queen. The *Bremen* and her consort dominated the Atlantic trade from northern Europe to the United States until the emergence of the French *Normandie* in 1935, but they suffered as the 1930s advanced as a consequence of the Nazi regime's unpopularity.

On the outbreak of World War II, the *Bremen* and *Europa* were earmarked to support the planned invasion of Great Britain, Operation "Sea Lion," as troop carriers. When this failed to materialize, both ships, already painted in vivid camouflage colors, were laid up. The *Bremen* remained idle at Bremerhaven where she was destroyed by fire on March 16, 1941. Although, publicly, air attack was attributed as the cause, the fire was actually started by a crew member during a feud with a colleague.

Canberra (1961-1997)

Owner: P&O Line/Cruises
Type: Former passenger liner and converted cruise ship—2,198 passengers in two classes
Builder: Harland & Wolff, Belfast—Yard No 1621, launched March 1, 1960
Dimensions: 49,073 GRT; 820 ft/250 m LOA; 102 ft/31.1 m BOA
Machinery: Turbo-electric, twin screw

Celebrated as the peak of ocean liner travel to the Antipodes, the *Canberra* achieved notoriety in two other periods of her long and successful career. She was conceived in the late 1950s when the demand for passages to Australia from the United Kingdom was at an unprecedented level, justifying the commissioning of a liner of her dimensions with a maximum speed of 20 knots that could reduce significantly the passage duration from the 28 days it then took to complete. She was immediately distinctive, not least because of her revolutionary engines-aft design, which allowed the distribution of the passenger amenities on her open decks, and in the long uninterrupted public rooms designed in a way not previously possible. Popular too, *Canberra* maintained the scheduled service from Southampton to Sydney and Melbourne from her maiden voyage on June 2, 1961 throughout the 1960s and into the next decade.

But even she could not resist the erosion of the ocean passenger trade by commercial airliners and in 1973 she was converted for full-time cruising. Not immediately successful in her new role, she gradually established an enviable reputation and a loyal clientele that returned to her time and again. Conflict with Argentina, in 1982, over the disputed Falkland Islands, forced an interruption to the *Canberra*'s cruise itinerary when she was taken over as a unit of the South Atlantic Task Force. Dubbed the "Great White Whale" she attracted greater notoriety for being the only large troopship that penetrated deep into the war zone. Amazingly, following a complete refit after return to her owners, the *Canberra* resumed her cruise duties and continued in the work for another 16 years. She was finally sold for breaking up in Pakistan in October 1997.

The *Carnival Destiny*-class

Owner: Carnival Cruise Line

Carnival Destiny (1996-)

Type: Active cruise ship—3,336 berths
Builder: Fincantieri, Monfalcone—Yard No 5941, launched March 1996
Dimensions: 101,353 GRT; 893 ft/272.2 m LOA; 118 ft/36.0 m BOA
Machinery: Diesel-electric, twin screw

LEFT, ABOVE LEFT & OVERLEAF: *Canberra*'s long and useful career included many prosperous years operating between the UK and the Antipodes, as well as general cruising and a stint as a troop carrier during the Falklands Crisis.

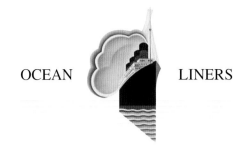

Carnival Triumph (1999-)

Type: Active cruise ship—3,473 berths
Builder: Fincantieri, Monfalcone—Yard No 5979
Dimensions: 101,509 GRT; 895 ft/273.0 m LOA; 118 ft/36.0 m BOA
Machinery: Diesel-electric, twin screw

Carnival Victory (2000-)

Type: Active cruise ship—c. 3,300 berths
Builder: Fincantieri, Monfalcone—Yard No 6045
Dimensions: 101,350 GRT; 892 ft/272.0 m LOA; 118 ft/36.0 m BOA
Machinery: Diesel-electric, twin screw

Carnival Conquest (2002-)

Type: Cruise ship under construction—c. 3,300 berths
Builder: Fincantieri, Monfalcone—Yard No 6057
Dimensions: 101,000 GRT; 892 ft/272.0 m LOA; 118 ft/36.0 m BOA
Machinery: Diesel-electric, twin screw

Carnival Glory (2003-)

Type: Cruise ship under construction—c. 3,300 berths
Builder: Fincantieri, Monfalcone—Yard No 6058
Dimensions: 101,000 GRT; 892 ft/272.0 m LOA; 118 ft/36.0 m BOA
Machinery: Diesel-electric, twin screw

Celebrated as the first passenger ships to exceed to the 100,000 gross registered tons barrier, the *Carnival Destiny* and her sisters are potent symbols of the explosive expansion of the ocean cruise business as well as of the massive growth of Carnival Cruise Line which now ranks with Royal Caribbean Cruise Line as one of the two largest operators in the industry.

By the time the *Carnival Victory* entered service in 2000 there were six 100,000 tons plus cruise ships in service, although these ships remain part of what is a select but growing club of super-cruise vessels which, by 2004, will have increased to some 19 ships of this size.

From Carnival's point of view they form part of an ambitious strategic investment program costing $2.1 billion under which eight new cruise vessels would be commissioned between 1995 and 2000. Subsequent deliveries will take the cost of this new building and expansion program even higher. Ships of this scale have taken the cruising vessel from "floating hotel" to "floating resort" status. Although their overall length still falls below that of the longest passenger liners ever built, they are marginally wider but considerably taller or deeper from keel to top of the superstructure. The 12 decks of the *Carnival Destiny*-class are so high that passengers on the topmost level would look down on the Statue of Liberty. At such dimensions, stability dictates a broader beam which

will mean that these vessels will be the first of their kind that are incapable of passing through the Panama Canal.

Half the passenger cabins are outside, of which 60 percent have balconies overlooking the sea. The range of accommodation includes a small number of luxury penthouse suites. With passenger cabins that tend to be larger than the industry standard, the space ratio of these giants is 38.30 at an occupancy level of approximately 2,800 passengers. Delivered in the spring of 1996, the *Carnival Destiny* was joined by the *Carnival Triumph* in 1999 and the *Carnival Victory* a year later. The *Carnival Triumph* experienced an unexpected delay to her entry into service when one of her propeller shafts overheated and her maiden voyage had to be cancelled. The *Carnival Destiny* experienced engine failure twice in the 2000 season, first in February and then again on May 23, during a visit to Boston. Her next scheduled cruise had to be abandoned.

Carnival Cruise Line operates mainly in the Caribbean and Alaskan circuits, offering superior quality all-American style holidays with lots of "pazazz." Known for their lively atmosphere, they are aimed at the seriously energetic cruise-maker. The standard of service aboard Carnival ships is excellent.

BELOW: With well over 3,000 berths the *Carnival Destiny* is a testament to the success of Carnival Cruise Lines as well as the public's return to the sea in search of rest and relaxation.

Celebration
see the *Holiday*-class

The *Century*-class
Owner: Celebrity Cruises

Century (1995-)
Type: Active cruise ship—1,866 berths
Builder: Meyer Werft, Papenburg—Yard No 637
Dimensions: 70,606 GRT; 815 ft/248.5 m LOA; 105 ft/32.0 m BOA
Machinery: Diesel, twin screw

Galaxy (1996-)
Type: Active cruise ship—1,896 berths
Builder: Meyer Werf, Papenburgt—Yard No 638

Dimensions: 76,522 GRT; 866 ft/263.9 m LOA; 105 ft/32.0 m BOA
Machinery: Diesel, twin screw

Mercury (1997-)

Type: Active cruise ship—1,890 berths
Builder: Meyer Werft, Papenburg—Yard No 639
Dimensions: 77,713 GRT; 866 ft/263.9 m LOA; 106 ft/32.0 m BOA
Machinery: Diesel, twin screw

Celebrity Cruises, whose origins can be traced back to the Chandris Lines, which once operated scheduled services from Europe to Australasia, is now a subsidiary of the Royal Caribbean Cruise Lines group. The *Century* was their third newly-constructed cruise ship and the first of a series of 70,000 gross tons plus vessels.

The *Century* was the first of the trio to enter service, joining smaller fleet-mates *Horizon* and *Zenith,* which had been produced by the same German shipyard. After a brief promotional call at Southampton, the *Century* commenced year-round cruising from Port Everglades with her maiden departure on December 20, 1995. Her program of cruises are promoted in the United Kingdom as fly cruises of nine and 16 day duration.

Second ship of the trio, the *Galaxy*, was delivered on October 10, 1996. Just over a year later on October 15, 1997, the *Mercury*, which had been laid down May 29, 1996, was handed over to her owners at the end of acceptance trials, in a festive ceremony that took place at Eemshaven in the Netherlands, thereby completing the three ship order. The *Century*-class ships constituted the largest passenger ships built in Germany up to that time.

ABOVE FAR LEFT: Celebrity Cruises' *Galaxy*, launched in 1996 with a GRT of 76,522 has capacity for 1,896 passengers.

ABOVE LEFT: *Galaxy*'s casino.

LEFT: Also in the Celebrity Cruises fleet is the slightly more recent *Mercury*, launched in 1997.

Accommodation and machinery aboard these vessels is stylish and innovative. For their size they carry a relatively low passenger complement, reflected in a space ratio of over 40.0. The majority of cabins are of the outside type, with their own balconies, and each offers a small number of extremely luxurious private suites. Among the passenger facilities aboard each is a three-deck high atrium positioned aft, a two-tiered main restaurant capable of serving around 1,100 guests at a single sitting and an observation lounge with seating for just under half as many passengers again.

The configuration of the main diesel engines is interesting, comprising two nine-cylinder greater output units coupled with two six-cylinder less powerful units. The arrangement is designed to provide operational flexibility, permitting adjustment to be made to suit varying conditions of weather and seaway.

These highly graded cruise ships follow the pattern of the Celebrity fleet as a whole, being mainly centered in the Caribbean and Latin American regions in the winter while, during the summer months cruise tours are offered in the Mediterranean, to Alaska, and along the eastern coastline of the United States.

Conte Di Savoia (1932-1943)

Owner: Italia Line—ex *Dux* ex *Conte Azzuro*
Type: Former passenger liner—2,200 passengers in four classes
Builder: Cantieri Ruiniti dell'Adriatico, Trieste—Yard No 783, launched October 28, 1931
Dimensions: 48,502 GRT; 860 ft/262.2 m LOA; 96 ft/29.3 m BOA
Machinery: Steam turbines, quadruple screw

As the consort to the *Rex*, Italy's one and only Atlantic Blue Riband record holder, the *Conte Di Savoia's* greatest claim to fame was her autogyro stabilizer installation designed to reduce rolling and improve passenger comfort in a rough seaway. She was, in fact, quite unlike her fleet-mate for the two vessels had only come together as a result of an Italian Government

inspired amalgamation. The *Rex* had been conceived as a Navigazione Generale Italiana ship, the *Conte Di Savoia* having begun life on the drawing boards to the account of Lloyd Sabaudo. Neither ship sailed for their original owners as the merger was completed before either entered service. The *Conte Di Savoia*'s maiden voyage was a calamitous affair, dogged by technical difficulties that at one point put her continued safety in jeopardy.

Thereafter, with repairs fully effected, she settled into a smooth pattern of sailings enjoying the popular-ity that was exclusive to the "sunny southern route" from the Mediterranean to New York. When Italy entered World War II, in the summer of 1940, she was laid up amid vague rumors of conversion for auxiliary employment. This did not transpire, however, and she remained idle, moored near Venice, until September 1943, when Allied aircraft attacked her. Further damage from later raids left her totally destroyed and after the War's end her unrecognizable remains were broken up for scrap.

ABOVE LEFT: The *Conte Di Savoia* regularly plied the warmer waters of the Atlantic between the Mediterranean and New York before World War II.

LEFT: A 1930s advertising poster for the Italia Line.

ABOVE: The most recent liner to join the Costa fleet, and the largest, *Costa Atlantica* is to be followed into service by a sister-ship in 2003.

Costa Atlantica (2000-)

Owner: Costa Cruises
Type: Active cruise ship—2,112 berths
Builder: Kvaerner Masa—Yard No 498
Dimensions: 85,700 GRT; 958 ft/292.0 m LOA; 105 ft/32.0 m BOA
Machinery: Diesel-electric, twin screw

Costa Cruises is another passenger shipping company with a long heritage extending back to the days of scheduled passenger liner operations. Today its cruise operation forms yet another part of the Carnival Corporation conglomerate. Costa vessels alternate between the Mediterranean in summer, and Central America and the Caribbean in winter.

The *Costa Atlantica* is the latest and largest addition to the company's cruise fleet. She entered service in the summer of 2000.

A sister ship to the *Costa Atlantica* has been ordered from the same Finnish builders for delivery in spring 2003. They will be followed by two much larger, 105,000 gross ton vessels that were ordered simultaneously from Fincantieri's subsidiary yard of Sestri Cantiere Navale in Italy.

The *Costa Classica*-class

Owner: Costa Cruises

Costa Classica (1991-)

Type: Active cruise ship—1,905 increased to 2,485 berths

Builder: Fincantieri, Venice—Yard No 5877, floated February 2, 1991

Dimensions: 52,926 GRT; 730 ft/222.6 m LOA; 105 ft/32.0 m BOA—as built

85,000 GRT; 876 ft/267.2 m LOA; 105 ft/32.0 m BOA—as stretched

Machinery: Diesel, triple screw (twin screw—as built)

Costa Romantica (1993-)

Type: Active cruise ship—1,905 increased to 2,485 berths

Builder: Fincantieri—Yard No 5899

Dimensions: 53,049 GRT; 731 ft/223.0 m LOA; 105 ft/32.0 m BOA—as built

85,000 GRT; 875 ft/267.0 m LOA; 105 ft/32.0 m BOA—as stretched

Machinery: Diesel, triple screw (twin screw—as built)

Completed in October 1991 and in 1993 respectively, Costa announced plans in 1998 to have the *Costa Classica* and the *Costa Romantica* stretched by over 100 feet to increase their occupancy level by 30 percent. (Some trade papers put their new size at a somewhat lower 79,000 gross registered tons). The modifications include enhancements to their power plants and the addition of a third propeller in order to increase their service speed. Work on the *Costa Classica* was due to take until March 2001, assuming commencement in November 2000 after her new mid section had been built by Cammell Laird, Birkenhead, with whom the contract for the enlargement work had been placed. The operation made the headlines late in 2000 when it became apparent that Costa Cruises were in dispute with the shipyard concerning the £51 million contract. The *Costa Classica's* owners dramatically ordered that the movement of the ship from Italy to the River Mersey was not to take place as scheduled and the press were notified that the contract had been suspended. The new mid-body extension was launched on November 27, a day later than planned, because of high winds. Tugs then towed it to the yard's wet basin where it has been secured ever since pending the next stage of the operation.

Modifications to the *Costa Romantica* will commence as soon as the work on the *Costa Classica* is complete but when that will be is anyone's guess at the time of going to press. There are no indications as to how resolution of the problem is progressing. Meanwhile, the *Costa Classica* remains idle at Genoa where she has been laid up since the day when her new mid-body section was launched.

Prior to their enlargement, this Costa pair already had a more than reasonable space ratio of approximately 40.0 and it is anticipated that this will increase,

ABOVE RIGHT: The *Costa Allegre* **is a converted container ship.**

RIGHT & OVERLEAF: The new ships show clean, spare lines, though the distinctive cluster of buff funnels with a narrow blue band toward the stern remain.

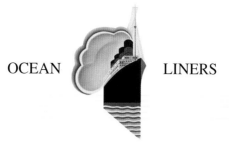

even though the main purpose of the jumboisation treatment, whenever it is eventually finalized, is to increase overall occupancy levels. Costa ships are known for their individuality of character and style, qualities reflected in the *Costa Classica* and *Costa Romantica* which are sister ships in tonnage and dimensions alone, as are the classmates of most fleets.

The *Costa Classica* had an embarrassing experience in 1997 when an anchor failure off the Greek island of Kythira left her in a very precarious situation. Local tugs went to the rescue, securing the cruise ship until the technical fault was remedied.

Costa Victoria (1996-)

Owner: Costa Cruises
Type: Active cruise ship—2,200 berths
Builder: Bremer Vulkan, Vegesack—Yard No 1107
Dimensions: 75,166 GRT; 830 ft/252.9 m LOA; 105 ft/32.0 m BOA
Machinery: Diesel-electric, twin screw

The *Costa Victoria* was ordered as one of two even larger passenger cruise ships for Costa Cruises from the Bremer Vulkan shipyard, as their second generation of purpose built vessels. However, when Bremer Vulkan got into difficulties the second ship, *Costa Olympia*, was left incomplete and eventually was finished to a revised specification for Norwegian Cruise Lines (see *Norwegian Sky*). Costa themselves made efforts to secure the partly-built hull to allow construction to proceed elsewhere, but were unsuccessful in this. Thus, the *Costa Victoria* has been left a one-off ship in the Costa fleet.

The *Costa Victoria* was fitted out in characteristic fashion, reflecting the classical stylishness long associated with Costa. The passenger space ratio is slightly lower than that of her two fleet-mates scheduled for stretching, a margin that will undoubtedly increase after the rebuilt ships have returned to service.

The *Costa Victoria* fits in with the Costa worldwide cruise operation, positioned according to seasonal adjustments.

The *Crown Princess*-class

Owner: Princess Cruises

Crown Princess (1990-)

Type: Active cruise ship—1,900 berths
Builder: Fincantieri, Monfalcone—Yard No 5839, floated May 25, 1989
Dimensions: 69,845 GRT; 804 ft/245.1 m LOA; 105 ft/32.0 m BOA
Machinery: Diesel-electric, twin screw

Regal Princess (1991-)

Type: Active cruise ship—1,784 berths
Builder: Fincantieri, Monfalcone—Yard No 5840, floated March 29, 1990
Dimensions: 69,845 GRT; 804 ft/245.0 m LOA; 105 ft/32.0 m BOA
Machinery: Diesel-electric, twin screw

For a time the largest ship in either the Princess or the combined P&O/Princess fleets of cruising vessels, the *Crown Princess* was the lead ship in what turned out to be an ambitious six vessel building program, executed in two phases, embarked upon by P&O.

Originally ordered by Sitmar Cruises in 1987, the ship reverted to P&O in 1988 when they acquired the Italian concern. The *Crown Princess* was floated out of her building docks on May 25, 1989, and was delivered to her owners a year later on June 29, 1990. Her first cruise, in the Mediterranean, began on July 9, 1990, following which she transferred to New York and then to the Caribbean after just one call at Southampton, on September 13, 1990.

Her sister-ship is the *Regal Princess* which joined her a year later, in August 1991, after successful completion of acceptance trials. Since then, the *Crown*

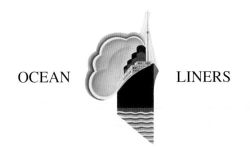

Princess and *Regal Princess* have been engaged continuously on Caribbean cruises out of Miami. Using the space ratio measurement applied to all modern cruise ships to show comparative allocation of shipboard space per passenger, this pair measure up at 43.9, a generous provision.

Along with all Princess vessels, the *Crown Princess* and *Regal Princess* are graded as premium standard, participating in an operation which, according to the seasons, offers sailings to all of the world's major cruise areas.

The *Regal Princess* suffered an unfortunate outbreak of gastrointestinal illness that affected over 300 passengers during June 1998, when she was cruising out of Vancouver. She was taken out of service temporarily for cleansing. The experience was horribly reminiscent of an incident involving the P&O ship *Oronsay* when a similar outbreak of stomach illness led to that ship being quarantined outside of Vancouver in 1969. Though such incidents are rare, it serves as a reminder that modern passenger ships can still be the victim of the old scourges of fire, disease, mechanical failure, and extreme weather.

LEFT: Princess Cruises' *Crown Princess* **is the first ship in a six vessel group of two sub-classes and has now been in continuous operation for over a decade.**

BELOW LEFT: Fleetmate of the *Crown* **and** *Regal Princess* **this is an aeriel view of the** *Grand Princess*.

BELOW: *Crystal Harmony* **is the largest passenger liner ever built in Japan and is widely considered to be one of the most luxurious vessels afloat.**

Crystal Harmony (1990-)

Owner: Crystal Cruises (Nippon Yusen Kaisha)
Type: Active cruise ship—960 berths
Builder: Mitsubishi Heavy Industries, Nagasaki—Yard No 2100, launched September 30, 1989
Dimensions: 48,621 GRT; 787 ft/241.0 m LOA; 98 ft/30.0 m BOA
Machinery: Diesel-electric, twin screw

But for the intervention of World War II, Japan would have completed its first two large passenger ships for Nippon Yusen Kaisha in the early 1940s, for the conveyance of the many American citizens expected to visit the Tokyo Olympic Games scheduled for 1940, which in the event were also abandoned.

Fifty years later, the *Crystal Harmony* emerged as the largest passenger ship ever built in Japan for cruise service with Crystal Cruises, itself a wholly owned subsidiary of Nippon Yusen Kaisha. The *Crystal Harmony* was delivered to her owners in July 1990 and commenced cruising from US ports, sailing to a variety of destinations.

Her success persuaded Crystal Cruises to supplement the operation with a second, similar, ship that entered service as the *Crystal Symphony* in 1995. With her consort, the *Crystal Harmony* is among the highest graded cruise ships for quality in the industry with a quite exceptional passenger space ratio of over 50. The pair are considered to be the best of the larger resort type cruise ships.

Crystal Symphony (1995-)

Owner: Crystal Cruises (Nippon Yusen Kaisha)
Type: Active cruise ship—975 berths
Builder: Kvaerner Masa, Turku—Yard No 1323
Dimensions: 51,044 GRT; 781 ft/238.0 m LOA; 105 ft/32.0 m BOA
Machinery: Diesel-electric, twin screws

So successful was the operation of the cruise ship *Crystal Harmony* that her owners opted for an almost identical companion vessel that joined her five years later, in April 1995. An order for a third, even larger ship from Chantiers de L'Atlantique was announced in 2000, for delivery in 2003.

Unusually, although the earlier *Crystal Harmony* was built in a Japanese shipyard, Crystal selected Kvaerner Masa in Finland to construct the follow-on vessel. The *Crystal Symphony* is generally very

ABOVE, ABOVE RIGHT & RIGHT: *Crystal Symphony* was ordered by Crystal Cruises after the success of her older sister-vessel, *Crystal Harmony*.

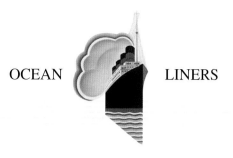

OCEAN   LINERS

similar, despite her different origins, benefiting from enhancements identified in the operation of the lead ship, including the repositioning of some of the public rooms.

Like her consort, the *Crystal Symphony* features a striking hand-cut glass waterfall in her two deck atrium-cum-plaza reception area. Both ships are rated as five star plus, offering generous passenger space and sumptuous accommodation of the highest standard. Over 50 percent of the staterooms and cabins have verandahs.

The *Crystal Symphony* launched her career with a promotional visit to Tilbury on April 21, 1995, en route to New York during her delivery voyage. Her employment involves cruising to Alaska and Canada in summer, moving to the Far East and Australasia for the rest of the year. Crystal Cruises' program of excursions includes an annual 96 day world cruise.

Dawn Princess
see the *Sun Princess*-class

The *Disney Magic*-class
Owner: Disney Cruise Vacations

Disney Magic (1998-)
Type: Active cruise ship—2,500 berths
Builder: Fincantieri, Venezia—Yard No 5989, launched April 17, 1997
Dimensions: 83,338 GRT; 964 ft/294.0 m LOA; 105 ft/32.0 m BOA
Machinery: Diesel-electric, twin screw

BELOW: *Disney Wonder* **is one of two ships that represent the famous entertainment company's entrance into the luxury cruise market.**

Disney Wonder (1999-)

Type: Active cruise ship—2,500 berths
Builder: Fincantieri, Venezia—Yard No 5990
Dimensions: 83,308 GRT; 964 ft/294.0 m LOA;
105 ft/32.0 m BOA
Machinery: Diesel-electric, twin screw

It had long been hinted that a major player from the film entertainment industry was planning to enter the cruise business, a logical enough extension of their leisure business interests. Speculation surrounded MGM until that organization's collapse, but when Disney announced its intentions to build, initially, two luxury cruise ships, it was immediately obvious that they were the ideal candidate for such a development, their cartoon character theme readily migrating to a shipboard leisure environment. Disney took initial steps to invest in vessel ownership in June 1994, in order to be part of the cruise industry's growth. Executives declared that cruise ships were a natural extension of their core business (there had been a short-lived affiliation with Premier Cruise Line prior to this). The result was two of the most stylish, distinctively individual cruise ships of recent times. They are the largest passenger ships operated by an American company, exceeding the tonnage of the old *United States* by a significant margin, if not her overall length.As might be expected the Mickey Mouse character, probably the most famous and most enduring Disney icon, is displayed on the sides of the twin funnels. Unlike many modern cruise ships, the other

BELOW: *Disney Wonder*, with her distinctive Mickey Mouse logos on the funnels, combines modern technology with the best of liner tradition and offers a unique cruising experience.

exception being those of Holland-America Line, their hulls are dark, embellished with delicate gold scroll-work. Interestingly, Disney had, prior to construction, declared its intentions to make its ships a reminder of the great age of the passenger liner and in this they have succeeded.

Emphasis onboard is on fun, with large areas devoted exclusively to children and teenagers. Cabins are of generous size (space ratio is 48.2), over 70 percent being placed on the outside of the hull and, of these, the majority have their own verandahs. All passenger accommodation, including standard inside cabins have a daytime sitting area. The Disney pair are not just gimmicky "floating funfairs". They are luxurious and stylish ships in their own right, combining all the classic features associated with the modern cruise ship (although there are no casinos or observation lounges), with elegant amenities that evoke the great age of passenger travel at sea, such as the three deck high entrance lobby with traditional grand staircases.

Technology has also been heavily exploited as exemplified in one restaurant, where, using light and sound media, the room transforms from black and white decor into full color with huge animations as the meal proceeds.

Disney Magic and *Disney Wonder* were delivered late due to problems of overloaded capacity at the shipyard, the latter entering service in the summer of 1999. Both support a seven-day Disney holiday package comprising short cruises from Port Canaveral to Nassau, Bahamas, alternating with a similar duration stay at Disney's Florida resort. They are unquestionable market leaders in the "themed" cruise sector, a dimension of the business which is set to becoming a dominant trend in future ocean cruising.

Ecstacy
see the *Fantasy*-class

Elation
see the *Fantasy*-class

Empress Of Britain (1931-1940)

Owner: Canadian Pacific Line
Type: Former passenger liner and cruise ship—1,195 passengers in three classes
Builder: John Brown, Clydebank—Yard No 530, launched June 11, 1930
Dimensions: 42,348 GRT; 760 ft/231.8 m LOA; 97 ft/27.9 m BOA
Machinery: Steam turbines, quadruple screw

When viewed retrospectively against the modern ocean passenger scene, dominated by its dedicated cruise ships, the pre-war *Empress Of Britain* makes a very interesting ship, for she was designed specifically to fulfil the dual roles of scheduled service liner on the Quebec run and luxury cruise ship for the winter season when the St. Lawrence Seaway was frozen over. The novel layout of her passenger cabins was developed with this twin functionality in mind and, in another novel diversion from established practice, two of her four propellers were detachable to permit a more sedate and efficient cruising speed while engaged on excursions. As such she represents, along with a very select few similar ships, a bridge between the out-and-out regular service liner and the purpose-built cruise ships of today.

The *Empress Of Britain* proved to be a success in both respects, among her achievements being the speed record on the transatlantic route from Southampton to Montreal. At the outbreak of World War II she was taken over as a troopship but her war service was short-lived. On October 26, 1940, she was attacked first by a German aircraft, northwest of Ireland, before succumbing to the torpedoes of a prowling U-boat two days later. Engulfed in flames she keeled over and sank with the loss of 49 lives from among her crew and complement.

ABOVE RIGHT & RIGHT: *Empress of Britain* **was a unique vessel, her design allowing her to operate as both scheduled service liner and luxury cruiser. Sadly, she was sunk early in World War II by a German U-boat.**

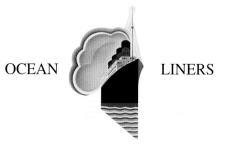

OCEAN LINERS

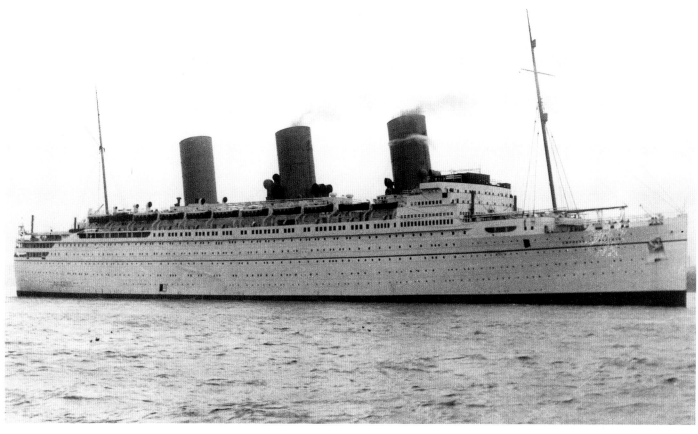

Enchantment Of The Seas
see the *Legend Of The Seas*-class

Explorer Of The Seas
see the *Voyager Of The Seas*-class

The *Fantasy*-class
Owner: Carnival Cruise Line

Fantasy (1990-)
Type: Active cruise ship—2,634 berths
Builder: Wartsila A/B and Masa Yards, Helsinki—Yard No 479, floated December 9, 1988
Dimensions: 70,367 GRT; 859 ft/262.0 m LOA; 105 ft/32.0 m BOA
Machinery: Diesel-electric, twin screw

Ecstacy (1991-)
Type: Active cruise ship—2,634 berths
Builder: Masa Yards, Helsinki—Yard No 480, floated October 21, 1989
Dimensions: 70,367 GRT; 859 ft/262.0 m LOA; 105 ft/32.0 m BOA
Machinery: Diesel-electric, twin screw

Sensation (1993-)
Type: Active cruise ship—2,634 berths
Builder: Kvaerner Masa, Helsinki—Yard No 484
Dimensions: 70,367 GRT; 858 ft/261.6 m LOA; 105 ft/31.4 m BOA
Machinery: Diesel-electric, twin screw

Fascination (1994-)
Type: Active cruise ship—2,624 berths
Builder: Kvaerner Masa—Yard No 487, floated October 21, 1989
Dimensions: 70,367 GRT; 855 ft/260.8 m LOA; 105 ft/32.0 m BOA
Machinery: Diesel-electric, twin screw

BELOW: Fifth in the eight-vessel *Fantasy*-class, the *Imagination* was launched in 1990.

Imagination (1995-)

Type: Active cruise ship—2,634 berths
Builder: Kvaerner Masa—Yard No 488
Dimensions: 70,367 GRT; 855 ft/260.8 m LOA; 105 ft/32.0 m BOA
Machinery: Diesel-electric, twin screw

Inspiration (1996-)

Type: Active cruise ship—2,634 berths
Builder: Kvaerner Masa—Yard No 489
Dimensions: 70,367 GRT; 855 ft/260.6 m LOA; 105 ft/32.0 m BOA
Machinery: Diesel-electric, twin screw

Elation (1998-)

Type: Active cruise ship—2,634 berths
Builder: Kvaerner Masa—Yard No 491
Dimensions: 70,367 GRT; 859 ft/262.1 m LOA; 105 ft/32.0 m BOA
Machinery: Diesel-electric, twin propulsion units

BELOW: Carnival Cruise Line's *Elation*, launched in 1998.

Paradise (1998-)

Type: Active cruise ship—2,634 berths
Builder: Kvaerner Masa, Turku—Yard No 494
Dimensions: 70,367 GRT; 855 ft/260.8 m LOA; 105 ft/32.0 m BOA
Machinery: Diesel-electric, twin propulsion units

The largest and most ambitious passenger-ship building program embarked upon by a single company, the *Fantasy*-class comprises eight vessels each of 70,000 gross registered tons. Alone they represent a greater tonnage than all of the giant passenger liners together that were introduced by all operators on the North Atlantic run between the World Wars.

Name ship of the series, the *Fantasy* was started at the famous Wartsila shipyard in Helsinki but when that concern failed, on November 7, 1989, she was completed by their successors, Masa Yards. After floating in December 1988, trials commenced the following July prior to delivery on January 26, 1990. She was not christened at the time she was floated, the naming ceremony not taking place until August 26, 1989.

Second of the group, the *Ecstacy* was likewise not officially named at the time she was floated but six months later on May 11, 1991, after her arrival at New York following delivery to her owners. Her maiden cruise commenced on June 9, 1991.

The *Sensation*, the third vessel to be completed was handed over to Carnival Cruise Line on October 18, 1993, leaving Helsinki for Miami, her home port, five days later. She too was christened subsequent to her acceptance, at a ceremony at Miami that took place on November 13 of that year. A notable feature of these first three *Fantasy*-class vessels was their six-deck high atrium with glass-walled elevators, a facility incorporated into the design of the later ships.

As the 1990s progressed, subsequent ships of the series joined those already in service—the *Fascination* in 1994, the *Imagination* in 1995, the *Inspiration* in 1996, and, completing the group, the *Elation* and *Paradise* in 1998; the latter pair differing from their six predecessors by having different propulsion units. In fact the *Elation* was the first cruise vessel to have "Azipods," revolutionary drive systems that pull a ship rather than push it, installed in place of conventional screw propellers. Inevitably, as pioneers of this new form of propulsion, there have been teething problems. The most serious sequence of disruptions occurred during 2000 when the *Paradise* was afflicted by a malfunction on July 16, shortly after setting sail, which compelled a return to Miami. Her next four cruises were cancelled while repairs were carried out at Newport News, Virginia. Later in the year, in October, the *Elation*, which had been experiencing similar problems, was withdrawn from service as a precautionary measure for preventative maintenance.

A quite different problem hit the *Ecstacy* on July 20, 1998, when fire broke out, it is believed in the crew's laundry at the aft end, while she was off Miami. Her crew, with the assistance of local tugs managed to extinguish the fire, but around 60 persons had to be treated for the effects of smoke inhalation. The *Ecstacy* was towed into her home port the following day and, on July 24, she was moved to Newport News for permanent repairs to be carried out. It was

estimated that the damages amounted to $24 million, including the lost cruise revenue.

Space ratio levels on the eight *Fantasy*-class ships is 34.40, assuming occupancy of 2,200 passengers. Along with other Carnival Cruise ships, they are employed on a cruise circuit that takes in the Caribbean, Mexico, and Alaska.

Fascination
see the *Fantasy*-class

Grandeur Of The Seas
see the *Legend Of The Seas*-class

The *Grand Princess*-class
Owner: Princess Cruises

Grand Princess (1998-)
Type: Active cruise ship—3,300 berths
Builder: Fincantieri—Yard No 5956, launched May 22, 1997
Dimensions: 108,806 GRT; 951 ft/289.9 m LOA; 118 ft/36 m BOA
Machinery: Diesel-electric, twin screw

Golden Princess (2001-)
Type: Cruise ship under construction—c. 3,300 berths
Builder: Fincantieri—Yard No 6050
Dimensions: 110,000 GRT; 951 ft/290.0 m LOA; 118 ft/36 m BOA
Machinery: Diesel-electric, twin screw

Star Princess (2002-)
Type: Cruise ship under construction—c. 3,300 berths
Builder: Fincantieri—Yard No 6051
Dimensions: 110,000 GRT; 951 ft/290.0 m LOA; 118 ft/36 m BOA
Machinery: Diesel-electric, twin screw

The largest ships in the Princess cruise fleet, the *Grand Princess* and her three sisters (a fourth unnamed ship is also on order) are among a growing number of mega cruise vessels of over 100,000 GRT. Two even larger

ABOVE: *Grand Princess* **entering the popular cruise destination St. Thomas Harbour in the US Virgin Islands.**

ships are on order for Princess from the Mitsubishi Heavy Industries Shipyard in Japan for delivery in 2003 and 2004, while a passenger ship of similar size and configuration to the *Grand Princess* series is also under construction at Fincantieri for P&O Cruises.

These vessels are a far cry from the first Princess cruise ship, the 6,000 ton *Princess Patricia*, operated back in 1965 when the company was founded. The *Grand Princess*'s inaugural voyage, leaving Istanbul on May 26, 1998, took her to Barcelona. Thereafter she continued with a program of Mediterranean summer cruises, taking in the rugged Amalfi coast and the romantic backdrop of Venice. In the winter she transfers to the Caribbean, operating from Miami.

The *Golden Princess* is scheduled to join her in April 2001, followed by the *Star Princess* in 2002. The fourth vessel of this series will enter service in 2003. Until the entry into service of Royal Caribbean's *Voyager Of The Seas*, in November 1999, the *Grand Princess* was the largest cruise ship in the world, an

increasingly short-lived accolade as these vessels continue to grow in size. Luxuriously appointed, voyagers aboard the *Grand Princess* enjoy supreme comfort and style in the quality of her onboard facilities. She scores highly over contemporary ships, particularly in the provision of balconies and verandah terraces, a stipulation of more and more cruise holidaymakers. Of her total number of outside staterooms, 80 percent are equipped in this fashion, a greater number than on any other ship afloat, all of generous size and not restricted just to the top grades of accommodation. She is the first ocean passenger ship to boast a wedding chapel permitting those whose inclination is to marry in exotic surroundings to "tie the knot" at sea in real style. The chapel is complemented with appropriate reception facilities. The honeymoon is, of course, already taken care of. Among other design features of the *Grand Princess* are a three-deck-high, atrium-type Grand Plaza with lifts encased in an illuminated "bubbleator tube," a glass-walled nightclub suspended 150 feet above her stern and a virtual reality zone where passengers can make a synthetic submarine voyage through coral reefs.

The *Grand Princess* quartet fall below the 1,000 feet mark in terms of overall length, their huge size resulting from their immense height. They measure 201 feet from keel to the top of the funnel, higher then the Niagara Falls by some 34 feet. The *Grand Princess*-class are premium rated with a passenger space ratio of 41.80. As part of a growing fleet, already consisting of seven large ships, the majority of them over 70,000 gross tons, they reinforce Princess Cruises position as the third largest operator in the business.

The *Holiday*-class

Owner: Carnival Cruise Line

Holiday (1985-)

Type: Active cruise ship—1,794 berths
Builder: Aalborg Vaerft, Aalborg—Yard No 246, launched December 10, 1983
Dimensions: 46,052 GRT; 727 ft/221.6 m LOA; 92 ft/28.0 m BOA
Machinery: Diesel, twin screw

Jubilee (1986-)

Type: Active cruise ship—1,800 berths
Builder: Kockums A/B, Malmo—Yard No 596, floated October 26, 1985
Dimensions: 47,262 GRT; 737 ft/224.8 m LOA; 92 ft/28.0 m BOA
Machinery: Diesel, twin screw

Celebration (1987-)

Type: Active Cruise ship—1,896 berths
Builder: Kockums A/B, Malmo—Yard No 597, floated August 9, 1986
Dimensions: 47,262 GRT; 733 ft/223.4 m LOA; 92 ft/28.0 m BOA
Machinery: Diesel, twin screw

Despite minor differences between them, these three vessels comprise a distinct class of second generation cruise ships, introduced by Carnival Cruise Line from the summer of 1985. The lead ship was built in Denmark, while the second pair were contracted to Swedish shipbuilders, in both cases being the largest passenger ships ever to be built in these countries. The *Holiday* commenced builder's trials in January 1985. Six months later, on June 3, 1985, she was delivered to her owners following which she took up position at Miami for cruising in the Caribbean. Almost exactly a year later, the *Jubilee* entered service, making her first departure from Miami on July 6, 1986. Typically, the cruises of the *Holiday* and *Jubilee* took them to such destinations as Cozumel Island off the Mexican coast, Grand Cayman, and Ocho Rios Bay, Jamaica.

The trio was completed with the inauguration of the *Celebration* in February of the following year. At the time, these three ships were among the largest purpose-built cruise vessels in the world, exceeded in size only by those few converted remnants of former route passenger liners. Though trend-setters in their day, the *Holiday*-class trio are now rapidly being overtaken by the new generation of cruise vessels currently entering service or under construction. This is reflected in their average passenger space ratio which, at just less than 32.0, is falling behind the standard of the industry's leading vessels. Likewise, the measure of their onboard facilities and amenities is now graded as moderate compared with the other ships of the Carnival fleet, all of which are graded as superior. Nevertheless, they still offer the impeccable passenger service for which Carnival is renowned.

On February 10, 1989, the two-year old *Celebration* was involved in a collision with the Cuban-flag cargo ship *Capitan San Louis*, 20 miles north of Punta Guérico, Venezuela. The Cuban ship broke in two and sank, costing the lives of three members of her crew. The damage to the *Celebration*, by comparison, was only slight and was soon rectified.

ABOVE RIGHT: *Jubilee* was the second liner in the *Holiday*-class and at the time of her launch was one of the largest liners afloat, though, like her sisters, she is now looking comparitively diminutive against a new generation.

RIGHT: *Celebration* is the last of three ships and proved the class's robustness after being relatively unharmed in a collision that broke the other ship in two.

The *Horizon*-class

Owner: Celebrity Cruises

Horizon (1990-)

Type: Active cruise ship—1,798 berths
Builder: Meyer Werft, Papenburg—Yard No 619, floated November 19, 1989
Dimensions: 46,811 GRT; 682 ft/208.0 m LOA; 95 ft/29.0 m BOA
Machinery: Diesel, twin screw

Zenith (1992-)

Type: Active cruise ship—1,730 berths
Builder: Meyer Werft, Papenburg—Yard No 620
Dimensions: 47,255 GRT; 682 ft/208.0 m LOA; 95 ft/29.0 m BOA
Machinery: Diesel, twin screw

The Celebrity Cruise ship *Horizon* was originally ordered by Fantasia Cruises, the first of a class of two stylish new vessels for cruises to the Bermuda Islands and in the Caribbean. She was christened in a

ABOVE: *Horizon*, the leader of her class, dwarfs the duty free shops at St. John's Quay, Antigua.

ABOVE RIGHT: The elegant Martini Bar onboard *Horizon*.

RIGHT: *Horizon*'s sister *Zenith*. Both liners are considered to offer a higher than an average level of comfort and style.

ceremony that took place on April 11, 1990, five months after she was floated out of her building berth at Papenburg and delivered to her owners on April 30, 1990. The second ship of the type, the *Zenith* joined the *Horizon* in 1992, working the same winter itinerary, the pair either summering in Europe or working the Alaska circuit. Celebrity's entry into the Alaskan cruise market was, in fact, inaugurated by the *Horizon* when she made her first cruise in this region in May 1996. Broadly similar in the range and layout of their accommodation, their passenger space ratios are moderate in both cases. They offer a premium product for the discerning traveler.

Ile De France (1927-1959)

Owner: Compagnie Générale Transatlantique (French Line)

Type: Former passenger liner—1,786 passengers later reduced to 1,345 passengers in three classes

Builder: Chantiers de L'Atlantique—Penhoét, St. Nazaire—Yard No R5, launched March 14, 1926

Dimensions: 44,356 GRT; 797 ft/243.0 m LOA; 92 ft/28.0 m BOA

Machinery: Steam turbines, quadruple screw

Where the contemporary *Bremen* introduced radical new exterior features to ocean passenger liner design, it was the *Ile De France* which set the trend in modern, stylish internal decor in the period between the wars. Her appointments were superb and she was

BELOW: The *Ile de France* operated successfully from her launch in 1926 until 1958. Renowned for her opulent furnishings and attractive interior design she was a very popular vessel.

ranked as one of the most attractively decorated and furnished liners of her generation, perhaps surpassed only by the *Normandie*, her later fleet-mate.

The *Ile De France* entered service on the North Atlantic run from Le Havre with her maiden voyage on June 22, 1927, continuing to make regular sailings, without interruption, until the outbreak of World War II. After the fall of France she was transferred under the management of Cunard White Star Line, operating as a troopship throughout the conflict. On the return of peace she was taken in hand for overhaul and renovation, a process which took longer than anticipated. When the *Ile De France* resumed the Atlantic passenger schedules on July 21, 1949, she had changed dramatically. In place of her original three funnels, two of broader profile had been substituted. To add to the illusion of a more modern external appearance, her hull was painted in a way that exaggerated the sheerline. Internally, she remained exceptional and her loyal following of the pre-war years flocked back to her.

The *Ile De France*'s post war operations finally ended in late 1958, when she was withdrawn from service and sold to shipbreakers in Osaka, Japan. Renamed *Furanzu Maru* for her final voyage, she was temporarily spared the cutter's torch when used as the setting for a Hollywood disaster movie in which she was sunk in shallow water as part of extravagantly staged scenes of realistic destruction.

Imagination
see the *Fantasy*-class

Inspiration
see the *Fantasy*-class

Jubilee
see the *Holiday*-class

The *Legend Of The Seas*
(Project Vision-class)

Owner: Royal Caribbean Cruise Line

Legend Of The Seas (1995-)
Type: Active cruise ship—2,060 berths, launched September 3, 1994
Builder: Chantiers de L'Atantique, St. Nazaire—Yard No A31
Dimensions: 69,130 GRT; 862 ft/262.7 m LOA; 105 ft/32.0 m BOA
Machinery: Diesel-electric, twin screw

Splendour Of The Seas (1995-)
Type: Active cruise ship—2,066 berths
Builder: Chantiers de L'Atantique, St. Nazaire—Yard No B31, launched June 17, 1995
Dimensions: 69,490 GRT; 867 ft/264.3 m LOA; 105 ft/32.0 m BOA
Machinery: Diesel-electric, twin screw

Grandeur Of The Seas (1996-)
Type: Active cruise ship—2,440 berths
Builder: Kvaerner Masa, Helsinki—Yard No 492

Dimensions: 73,817 GRT; 915 ft/279.1 m LOA; 105 ft/32.0 m BOA
Machinery: Diesel-electric, twin screw

Enchantment Of The Seas (1997-)
Type: Active cruise ship—2,430 berths
Builder: Kvaerner Masa, Helsinki—Yard No 493, launched November 21, 1996
Dimensions: 74,140 GRT; 915 ft/279.0 m LOA; 105 ft/32.0 m BOA
Machinery: Diesel-electric, twin screw

Rhapsody Of The Seas (1997-)
Type: Active cruise ship—2,416 berths
Builder: Chantiers de L'Atantique, St. Nazaire—Yard No E31
Dimensions: 78,491 GRT; 915 ft/279.0 m LOA; 105 ft/32.0 m BOA
Machinery: Diesel-electric, twin propulsion units

Vision Of The Seas (1998-)
Type: Active cruise ship—2,400 berths
Builder: Chantiers de L'Atantique, St. Nazaire—Yard No F31
Dimensions: 78,491 GRT; 915 ft/279.0 m LOA; 105 ft/32.0 m BOA
Machinery: Diesel-electric, twin propulsion units

Unusually referred to by the name of the last ship of the series rather than the first, the "Project Vision" or *Legend Of The Seas*-class was a development of the company's first three 70,000 gross ton vessels (see the *Sovereign Of The Seas*-class). This latter series in fact comprises three pairs having similar characteristics. The first two, the *Legend Of The Seas* and *Splendour Of The Seas*, built in France, featured the original concept of amidships funnel with the Royal Caribbean Cruise Line's hallmark Viking Crown panoramic lounge wrapped around the funnel structure. These were the smallest pair of the six. The following four ships were built to a modified design. Their funnels were placed aft and the Viking Crown lounge, in their case, was a detached structure placed

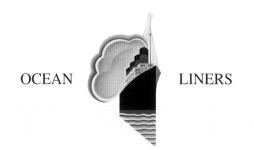

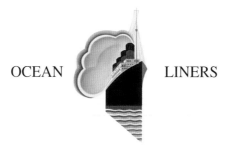

centrally on the upper deck. *Rhapsody Of The Seas* and *Vision Of The Seas*, the last ships of the series to be completed, and the largest of the six, were further distinguished by having "Podded" propulsion units installed in place of conventional screw propellers.

Glass has been used extensively in this class of ships allowing unhindered daylight into central areas and, conversely, free observation of the seascape from most public areas. Another distinctive feature is a seven-deck-high atrium with a parabolic glass ceiling. Access between decks is by means of exposed lifts that travel up and down the sides of the atrium. Over

LEFT: **The colorful casino onboard** *Vision of the Seas.*

BELOW LEFT: **The Project Vision-class delivers what the name promises. Extensive use of glass in the ships' design offers unparalleled views out onto the sea from public areas. This photograph of** *Grandeur of the Seas*, **taken at dusk, clearly shows the extent to which glass has been used.**

BELOW: *Enchantment of the Seas*, **launched in 1997, is one of the six vessels in the** *Project Vision*-**class.**

50 percent of the cabins are externally facing, the majority with their own balconies.

The *Legend Of The Seas* was delivered to her owners on April 29, 1995, commencing her maiden cruise on May 16 of that year. This took her from Miami to Los Angeles, via the Panama Canal, where she was to be based for a regular program of Alaska cruises. *Splendour Of The Seas* and *Grandeur Of The Seas*, the first of the Finnish-built duo, joined the lead-ship in service in 1996. The *Enchantment Of The Seas* arrived a year later, completing the group driven by screw propellers. In the *Rhapsody Of The Seas* and *Vision Of The Seas*, Royal Caribbean Cruise Lines adopted "Podded" propulsion units connected to the electric drive motors, a system which was also adopted by Carnival for its later *Fantasy*-class ships. Consideration was also given to equipping this pair with gas turbine-electric power-plants. Although operating costs would be higher for such installations, the compactness of size would have freed up space for

increased passenger accommodation. In the event, diesel-electric machinery was retained and the gas turbine experiment was reserved for the later *Radiance Of The Seas* and her "Project Vantage" series of sisters.

The "Vision"-class ships have generally experienced trouble-free operation. A relatively minor incident involved the *Grandeur Of The Seas* on October 31, 2000, when she lost all power for over four hours a short distance off the coast of Curacao. Tugs towed her to Willemstad where repairs were carried out.

Royal Caribbean employs the six "Project Vision" cruise ships in support of its broad program of worldwide excursions—mainly in the Caribbean in the winter months, but now extending to Asia and Australia. During the summer months operations extend to Europe, Alaska, and the eastern seaboard of the United States. The Fieldings Worldwide Cruises rating system grades them as five star. Passenger space ratios, depending on occupancy levels, average out at 38.5.

Leviathan (1914-1938)

Owner: United States Lines—ex *Vaterland* (1917)
Type: Former passenger liner—3,909 later reduced to 3,008 passengers in 3-4 classes
Builder: Blohm & Voss, Hamburg—Yard No 212, launched April 3, 1913
Dimensions: 59,955 GRT; 948 ft/289.2 m LOA; 100 ft/30.5 m BOA
Machinery: Steam turbines, quadruple screw

LEFT & BELOW LEFT: *Rhapsody of the Seas*, **which looks similar to her earlier siblings, but which has a very different propulsion system.**

BELOW: The *Leviathan*, **which began life as the German liner** *Vaterland*, **but was siezed by the US Government during World War I.**

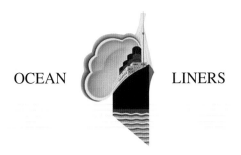

ABOVE: *Leviathan*'s fortunes failed to rise as a passenger liner operated during Prohibition, and after a dismal career she was demolished in Scotland.

The Hamburg-Amerika liner *Vaterland* saw less than six months of service on the Atlantic passenger route before she was interned at New York for almost the duration of World War I. In April 1917, on the United States' entry into the war, she was seized and converted into the troopship *Leviathan*. The American government retained her after the Armistice, restoring her as a passenger liner and placing her in service with the newly established United States Lines from June 1923. Unlike her former German fleet-mates, the *Leviathan* did not prove to be a particularly successful or profitable ship. She suffered for the lack of a consort of comparable speed and capacity, so that her owners struggled to maintain a balanced or regular schedule of sailings. The adverse impact of the United State's Prohibition laws, preventing the sale of alcoholic drinks aboard her, also did nothing to help improve her fortunes. Finally, beset with mechanical breakdowns she was laid up in September 1934.

After languishing in an idle state for 40 months, she was sold for demolition at Rosyth, Scotland, the first of the Hamburg-Amerika trio to suffer this fate. Like the *Berengaria* ex *Imperator*, the *Leviathan* made her final crossing of the Atlantic completely empty.

Liberté (1930-1962)

Owner: Compagnie Générale Transatlantique (French Line)—ex *Europa* (1946)

Type: Former passenger liner—2,024 later reduced to 1,513 passengers in 3-4 classes

Builder: Blohm & Voss, Hamburg—Yard No 479, launched August 15, 1928

Dimensions: 51,839 GRT; 941 ft/286.7 m LOA; 102 ft/31.1 m BOA

Machinery: Steam turbines, quadruple screws

ABOVE RIGHT & RIGHT: The *Liberté*, formerly the *Europa*, was renamed following her transfer to France after World War II. During her career she was sunk twice, but was salvaged both times.

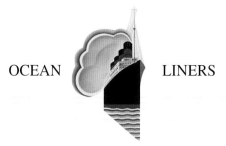

LEFT: Interior of the French liner *Liberté*, the First Class Grand Salon.

BELOW LEFT: The *Liberté* (ex *Europa*) at New York City's harbor.

Second of a pair of record breaking German liners commissioned in the inter-war period, the Norddeutscher Lloyd *Europa*'s entry into service was delayed when she was ravished by fire at the fitting-out quay. To save her, her builders were compelled to sink her on an even keel, permitting her to be subsequently refloated and repaired. Her maiden voyage commenced on March 19, 1930, and she immediately took the Atlantic Blue Riband westbound at a speed of 27.91 knots, later losing the honors to her sistership *Bremen* which achieved 28.51 knots in July 1933, during her fourth season.

After the outbreak of World War II, the *Europa* passed to the Kriegsmarine who commenced converting her for the planned Operation "Sea Lion." When this was abandoned, the great liner remained secured at her berth at Bremerhaven until the end of the war. United States' forces seized her there in May 1945, and she was immediately pressed into transport service, repatriating American servicemen. On the completion of this work, the United States authorities did not retain the *Europa*. Instead she was transferred to France as a replacement for the *Normandie*, which had been destroyed by fire in 1942.

Appropriately renamed *Liberté*, she was taken in hand for renovation but for the second time in her career she was forcibly sunk on an even keel after she was driven onto the wreck of the *Paris* during a violent storm at Le Havre in December 1946. The fully restored *Liberté* made her French Line debut on August 17, 1950, and immediately became one of the most popular liners on the Western Ocean in the post-war era.

A year before the new *France* entered service, in December 1961, the *Liberté*'s long career came to an end when she was sold to Italian ship breakers at La Spezia where she arrived in January 1962.

Maasdam
see the *Statendam*-class

Majestic (1902-1939)
Owner: White Star Line—ex *Bismarck* (1922)
Type: Former passenger liner—2,145 passengers in three classes
Builder: Blohm & Voss, Hamburg—Yard No 214, launched June 20, 1914
Dimensions: 56,620 GRT; 956 ft/291.5 m LOA; 100 ft/30.5 m BOA
Machinery: Steam turbines, quadruple screw

Largest of a trio of giant Atlantic liners planned by Albert Ballin, the president of the Hamburg-Amerika Line, the *Bismarck* was incomplete when World War I started. After the end of the war she was taken under the reparations conditions of the Treaty of Versailles and acquired by White Star Line as compensation for the loss of the *Britannic*, sister liner to the *Olympic* and *Titanic*. Though a matter of some delicacy, the *Bismarck* was completed at the Hamburg shipyard for her new British owners. She sailed for Liverpool, then Southampton in March 1922 where, upon her arrival, she was renamed *Majestic*. Despite a dubious claim by the United States Lines' *Leviathan*, the *Majestic* remained the largest passenger liner in the world until the advent of the *Normandie*.

From the beginning of 1934 she came under the ownership of the combined Cunard White Star Line, but there was no place for her in the merged fleet of these two great shipping companies, the older *Berengaria* being retained in preference. Laid up at Southampton in February 1936, she was destined for the breakers yard until the Admiralty stepped in and purchased her for use as a training and accommodation ship for boy cadets berthed at Rosyth, Scotland.

Renamed yet again and commissioned as HMS *Caledonia*, the former liner sailed north after conversion for her new role. The *Caledonia* was moved to moorings in the center of the River Forth on the

OCEAN LINERS

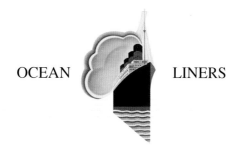
outbreak of World War II to provide some protection from aerial bombardment, but the ship was no safer in her new location. During an air attack on the night of September 29, 1940, she caught fire and was completely gutted. Her charred remains were dismantled where they lay, nothing remaining of her by the middle of 1943, when the remains of her wreck were raised and taken to Inverkeithing for final demolition.

LEFT & BELOW LEFT: White Star Line's *Majestic*, which was acquired, following World War I, as reparation for the loss of *Britannic*. For a time she was the largest passenger liner in the world.

BELOW: *Michelangelo* was another ship to have a less than sparkling career. Introduced specifically for the transatlantic trade at a time when it was rapidly being superceded by air travel, she was later damaged in a storm, then sold to Iran. After vanishing for a decade she ended her days at a Taiwanese breaker's yard.

Majesty Of The Seas
see the *Sovereign Of The Seas*-class

Mercury
see the *Century*-class

Michelangelo (1965-1991)

Owner: Italia Line

Type: Former passenger liner—1,775 passengers in three classes

Builder: Ansaldo SpA, Sestric Ponente—Yard No 1577, launched September 1962

Dimensions: 45,991 GRT; 906 ft/276.2 m LOA; 99 ft/30.1 m BOA

Machinery: Steam turbines, twin screw

One of the last two large passenger liners to be built primarily for scheduled service work on the North Atlantic, the *Michelangelo* made her first crossing on

the Genoa to New York route on May 12, 1965. Given the evident downturn that the trade was already experiencing, there were concerns about Italia Line's wisdom at introducing vessels of this type at such an inauspicious time. As if to vindicate these misgivings, the *Michelangelo* and her sister *Raffaello*, enjoyed only nine seasons on the Atlantic run, supplemented by occasional cruise voyages, before switching to full time cruising in 1974.

The *Michelangelo* was damaged in a fierce Atlantic storm on April 12, 1966. Two passengers and one crew member were killed when huge seas smashed her superstructure, a sobering reminder of the violent force of the ocean. After less than a year employed exclusively as a cruise ship, the *Michelangelo* was laid up, deemed unsuitable for this trade.

Eighteen months of idleness was ended when she was sold with her sister to the Government of Iran for conversion to naval accommodation ships stationed at Bandar Abbas, where she arrived on July 21, 1977. For almost a decade, the status of the *Michelangelo* and her sister was unknown, concealed behind the secrecy occasioned by the conflict between Iran and Iraq. Leaked stories suggested that they had been damaged in exchanges between land forces. In September 1986 it was reported that the much dilapidated former Italian luxury liner had been sold to Taiwanese breakers. As it turned out though, she was to linger for another five years, finally arriving at Karachi in July 1991 to be broken up.

The *Millennium*-class
Owner: Celebrity Cruises

Millennium (2000-)
Type: Active cruise ship—2,524 berths
Builder: Chantiers de L'Atlantique, St. Nazaire—Yard No R31
Dimensions: 91,000 GRT; 964 ft/294.0 m LOA; 105 ft/32.0 m BOA
Machinery: Gas turbine-electric, twin propulsion units

Infinity (2001-)
Type: Active cruise ship—c. 2,500 berths
Builder: Chantiers de L'Atlantique, St. Nazaire—Yard No S31
Dimensions: 91,000 GRT; 964 ft/294.0 m LOA; 105 ft/32.0 m BOA
Machinery: Gas turbine-electric, twin propulsion units

Summit (2001-)
Type: Cruise ship under construction
Builder: Chantiers de L'Atlantique, St. Nazaire—Yard No Y31
Dimensions: 91,000 GRT; 964.3 ft/294.0 m LOA; 105 ft/32.0 m BOA
Machinery: Gas turbine-electric, twin propulsion units

4th ship unnamed (2002-)
Type: Cruise ship under construction
Builder: Chantiers et Ateliers de L'Atlantique—Yard No U31
Dimensions: 91,000 GRT; 964 ft/294.0 m LOA; 105 ft/32.0 m BOA
Machinery: Gas turbine-electric, twin propulsion units

The appropriately named *Millennium*-class—the largest group of cruise ships now entering service that fall in size just below the 100,000 gross ton mark—are celebrated for the engine and propulsion system developments that they have pioneered. Royal Caribbean Cruise Lines, the owners of Celebrity Cruises, intimated that gas turbine powered electric drive engines would be adopted for this class as well as for the final units of the "Project Vision" series ships back in April 1998. With gas turbine-electric drive installations, higher fuel costs are offset by reductions in the manning levels of engine-room crews and the release of machinery space for the provision of additional passenger accommodation. Besides having this radical main power-plant system, the *Millennium*-class have

dispensed with conventional screw propellers and are the first vessels to be fitted instead with so-called "Mermaid" pods—multi-directional units, developed jointly by Alstom of France and Kamewa of Sweden. Attached to the underwater hull, they obviate the need for conventional steering gear. To add to the list of credits clocked up by the *Millennium*, when she visited Southampton in June 2000 she became, temporarily, the largest passenger ship ever to enter the port. The record was short-lived, however, being broken just four months later when Royal Caribbean Cruise Line's *Explorer Of The Seas* paid a call on October 3, 2000.

The *Millennium* is well provided for in the way of passenger amenities, as might be expected for the new flagship of a major operator. She is commodious and

BELOW: The aptly-named *Millennium*, launched in 2000, features pioneering propulsion technology called "Mermaid" pods.

elegant in her appointments, in keeping with the standards established with earlier fleet-mates. Larger than average cabins are a feature of her accommodation. Her owners sphere of operation will take her to the Caribbean and Panama during the winter season, switching to either the European or Alaskan circuits for the summer months.

The second ship of the *Millennium*-class, the *Infinity* is scheduled to enter service in February 2001, a month later than intended. Modifications had to be made to her stern to correct the excessive vibration that had been experienced by the *Millennium* during her first months of service. The *Millennium* herself was dry-docked simultaneously at New York to have the same structural alterations carried out. The third ship, the *Summit*, makes her debut in August 2001. Three further ships of this type are either on order or are the subject of contractual options, due to be commissioned between 2002 and 2004.

Mistral (1999-)

Owner: Festival Cruises
Type: Active cruise ship—1,196 berths
Builder: Chantiers de L'Atlantique, St. Nazaire—Yard No J31
Dimensions: 47,276 GRT; 708 ft/216.0 m LOA; 95 ft/29.0 m BOA
Machinery: Diesel-electric, twin screw

The *Mistral* is the first new ship to be built for Festival Cruises since its formation in 1994. She is now the largest passenger ship currently operating under the French flag and the largest since French Line's *France*

of 1962. She attracted acclaim early on through the extravagant, almost bizarre christening ceremony lavished upon her at her builder's yard. An enormous tricolor, draped across the entire ship—all 700 feet of her—was unveiled at the critical point! The *Mistral* made her first call at Southampton soon afterward, on June 27, 1999, en route to the Mediterranean, via a European promotional tour, where her cruise service is to be concentrated.

Apart from all the usual amenities, the *Mistral* appears to be focussed on the health conscious, featuring a range of fitness-biased passenger facilities. These include a thalassotherapy pool containing sea water at body temperature, a hydrotherapy spa bath, a number of thermal suites, and a fully equipped gymnasium. Festival Cruises emphasize informality, providing traditional cruising experiences visiting Classical Mediterranean locations. Two more ships of the size of the *Mistral* have been ordered by Festival from the same shipyard with deliveries due in 2002 and 2003.

BELOW: *Mistral* **is the perfect cruise liner for healthy holiday-makers—she contains a comprehensive range of health and fitness facilities including therapy pools and a fully equipped gymnasium.**

Monarch Of The Seas

see the *Sovereign Of The Seas*-class

Nordic Empress (1990-)

Owner: Royal Caribbean Cruise Line

Type: Active cruise ship—2,284 berths

Builder: Chantiers de L'Atlantique, St. Nazaire—Yard No G29, launched August 28, 1989

Dimensions: 48,563 GRT; 691 ft/210.8 m LOA; 102 ft/31.0 m BOA

Machinery: Diesel, twin screw

Ordered by Admiral Cruises with the name *Future Seas* intended for her, this ship was taken over by Royal Caribbean Cruise Line while still under construction and christened as the *Nordic Empress*,

BELOW: The *Nordic Empress* is the second smallest vessel in the fleet of her operators, the Royal Caribbean Cruise Line.

entering service on May 31, 1990. Compared to the other cruise ships in the Royal Caribbean fleet, the *Nordic Empress* is relatively small, in fact she is now the company's second smallest unit, having a lower general grading for amenities and quality of service, and a passenger space ratio of 30.2 which, by today's standards, is rather modest. The *Nordic Empress* operates on cruises to the Bahamas from Miami, as well as to other destinations.

Normandie (1935-1942)

Owner: Compagnie Générale Transatlantique (French Line)

Type: Former passenger liner—1,472 passengers in three classes

Builder: Chantiers de L'Atlantique—Penhet, St Nazaire—Yard No T6

Dimensions: 86,495 GRT; 1,029 ft/313.7 m LOA; 117.8 ft/35.9 m BOA

Machinery: Turbo-electric, quadruple screws

ABOVE: The beautifully designed and opulently furnished *Normandie* is a legendary liner. Her brief career ended in disaster during conversion to a troopship in World War II.

Probably the most stylish, most inspirational passenger liner ever built, the *Normandie* was unashamedly focussed on the prestigious end of the market, the greatest percentage of her passenger accommodation being in First Class. She was a quarter as big again as the *Bremen*, whose Atlantic Blue Riband crown she eclipsed with speeds of 29.98 knots westbound and 30.31 knots eastbound, but so balanced was her design that her massive proportions were concealed within an elegant, rakish hull and superstructure. Sadly, for such an evocative and celebrated ship, fate was to deprive her of the career she deserved and within seven years she was little more than a fading memory.

The *Normandie* commenced her maiden voyage from Le Havre on May 29, 1935. A year later, the introduction of Cunard Line's *Queen Mary* on the Atlantic run, heralded a brief period of intense but friendly rivalry between these classic liners, elevating public interest in the affairs of passengers ships to an

intensity not previously experienced. She regained the speed record with speeds of 30.58 knots outward bound and 31.2 knots for the return leg to Europe only to lose it again to the *Queen Mary* in August 1938. It was claimed that the *Normandie*, unlike her British counterpart, did not make money for her owners but these were untypical times and even as the decade closed, with the final months of peace, passenger numbers on the Atlantic service had still not returned to anything like their pre-Depression levels. No doubt, the imminent war had held up the recovery.

The *Normandie* was in New York when war broke out in Europe and, for her safety, she remained there. As France had already capitulated, when the United States entered the war in December 1941, the *Normandie* was taken over for conversion into the Navy troop transport *Lafayette*. Unfortunately, a hurried and disorganized modification program resulted in a calamitous blaze aboard the great ship that was compounded by a bungled fire-fighting effort. The hapless ship, destabilized by the volume of water pumped into her, rolled over onto her side and in and instant she changed from being the world's largest

ocean liner to the world's most challenging salvage project. By the time it was over the *Lafayette* had been dismembered down to her top deck and there was little justification for adding an equally expensive restoration to the already burdensome costs of the salvage operation. Ultimately, the French Line was financially compensated for her loss but even as this redress was being settled, the remains of the once beautiful *Normandie* were broken up. Scrapping began in October 1946, just a year after she was formally stricken from the list of US Navy ships.

Norway (1962-)

Owner: Norwegian Cruise Line—ex *France* (1979)
Type: Active converted passenger liner—2,400 berths
Builder: Chantiers de L'Atlantique, St. Nazaire—Yard No G19, launched May 11, 1960
Dimensions: 76,049 GRT; 1,035 ft/315.5 m LOA; 111 ft/34.0 m BOA
Machinery: Steam turbines, twin screw (quadruple screw as built)

The elegant *France* was one of the last superliners to be designed and constructed specifically for the North Atlantic scheduled passenger service, regrettably arriving on the scene when that trade was already in steep decline. Thus her career as a transatlantic liner was brief and ended abruptly when the operating subsidies on which she depended were withdrawn by the French Government.

Designed as a two-class ship, with the bulk of her accommodation in Tourist class, she did not exhibit the luxurious grandeur of her illustrious predecessors. Nevertheless, she was a magnificent, stylishly-appointed ship. She entered service in January 1962 with a preliminary cruise, making her maiden departure for New York from Le Havre on February 3, 1962.

Laid up 12 years later in September 1974, she remained idle until June 1979, when she was purchased by the Klosters organization for conversion into the largest cruise ship of her time, renamed *Norway*. Her function, initially, was to provide transfer transportation in a holiday atmosphere between Miami and her owner's private offshore vacation

BELOW: Initially intended for the transatlantic trade like *Michelangelo*, *Norway* has been successfully converted to the cruise trade and is a luxurious and popular vessel nearly 40 years after her launch.

OCEAN LINERS

island in the Caymans. Besides this, comprising the hotel accommodation moored off the coast, she featured as part of the overall resort experience and was equipped accordingly. With the appeal of her size and heritage, she remains a favorite.

A series of major overhauls and renovations have dramatically changed her appearance, size, and propulsion installation. Between September and October 1990 she had two additional decks, comprising 135 luxury cabins and suites, constructed above her existing top deck. Further extensive refits in 1993 and 1996 ensure that she satisfies all the new SOLAS (Safety of Life at Sea) regulations, extending her service life out into the future. The *Norway* continues

LEFT, BELOW LEFT & BELOW: Since being launced as *France*, *Norway* has had a number of major refits and is still a sumptuous vessel.

to be a steam turbine powered ship, unlike the *Queen Elizabeth 2*, which has had radical engine modifications, but her propellers have been reduced to two as high speed is no longer a requirement and operating costs have been significantly reduced by de-rating her in this fashion.

She still figures prominently as an important element of the Norwegian Cruise Line fleet, even as new purpose-built cruise ships are being introduced, some of even greater proportions. Until the commissioning of Cunard's *Queen Mary 2* or the *Sagittarius II*-class vessels ordered by Star Line, whichever comes first, the *Norway*'s record, as the largest passenger liner in service and ever built, already of 40 years duration, is perpetuated. The *Norway* experienced a turbo-charger fire in 1999, while entering Barcelona, which put her out of action for three weeks.

The *Norwegian Dream*-class
Owner: Norwegian Cruise Line

Norwegian Dream (1992-)
ex *Dreamward* (1998)

Type: Active cruise ship—1,750 increased to 2,100 berths

Builder: Chantiers de L'Atlantique, St. Nazaire—Yard No C30, launched February 24, 1992

Dimensions: 39,217 GRT; ? ft/ m LOA; 105 ft/32.0 m BOA—as built

50,760 GRT; 754 ft/230.0 m LOA; 105 ft/32.0 m BOA—as stretched

Machinery: Diesel, twin screw

BELOW: *Norwegian Dream*, **operated by Norwegian Cruise Line was involved in a serious accident at sea in 1999 when she collided with another ship.**

Norwegian Wind (1993-)
ex *Windward* (1998)

Type: Active cruise ship—1,750 increased to 2,100 berths

Builder: Chantiers et Ateliers de L'Atlantique—Yard No D30, launched 14 September 1992

Dimensions: 39,217 GRT; ? ft/m LOA; 105 ft/32.0 m BOA—as built

50,760 GRT; 754 ft/230.0 m LOA; 105 ft/32.0 m BOA—as stretched

Machinery: Diesel, twin screw

The sister ships *Norwegian Dream* and *Norwegian Wind* entered service in 1992 and 1993 as the *Dreamward* and *Windward* respectively, following the original naming convention of Norwegian Caribbean Cruise Lines, as their owner was then styled. Offering affordable cruises with that little bit extra, the two ships supported the company's broad spectrum of

cruise vacations, focussed on the Americas and renowned particularly for voyages to Alaska, Hawaii, South America, and Bermuda.

At the end of September 1997, the *Dreamward* experienced a technical malfunction which temporarily left her in a hazardous situation. An electrical fault shut down her main engines completely and left her drifting without power for 17 hours in the Gulf of St. Lawrence.

Some three to four years after they first entered service, the company contracted for them to be lengthened by the Lloyd Weft shipyard, to increase their capacity by 500 berths and to generally enhance their accommodation to meet higher passenger expectations. First into the shipyard for modifications was the *Windward* in October 1997. The *Dreamward*

BELOW: Like her sister, *Norwegian Wind* has been "stretched" to add extra accommodation and more comfort for today's discerning passengers.

followed her in March 1998. On completion of their respective stretches, the twin ships were renamed for return to service, the *Windward* becoming the *Norwegian Wind* and the *Dreamward* taking the new name *Norwegian Dream*. This was part of a general renaming policy in which all the company's ships, with the exception of the *Norway*, were given names beginning with "Norwegian."

In her second season, following the lengthening process, the *Norwegian Dream* was involved in a major incident when she collided with the container ship *Ever Decent* in the Dover Strait on August 23, 1999. The *Ever Decent* was the more seriously damaged of the two. A number of her ballast tanks were ruptured and she assumed a list. More serious still, the impact caused a quantity of paint in containers on her deck to catch fire and the blaze spread to the surrounding area. The ship burnt for seven days before the fire was extinguished. As for the *Norwegian Dream*, her bow was seriously crumpled but there

ABOVE: *Norwegian Majesty*, launched in 1992, has a GRT of 40,876 and capacity for 1,800 passengers.

were no injuries. She proceeded to Dover, to disembark her 2,338 passengers, and thence to the Lloyd Weft shipyard at Bremerhaven for repair, where she arrived on August 28.

Now fully restored, the *Norwegian Dream* and *Norwegian Wind* maintain a full schedule of cruises along with other Norwegian Cruise Line ships, working all the main destinations and itineraries. Post their major modifications they offer a passenger space ratio of 29.0 in four star superior-graded accommodation.

Norwegian Majesty (1992-)

Owner: Norwegian Cruise Line—ex *Royal Majesty* (1997)
Type: Active cruise ship—1,800 berths
Builder: Kvaerner Masa, Helsinki—Yard No ?
Dimensions: 40,876 GRT; 679 ft/207.0 m LOA; 92 ft/28.0 m BOA
Machinery: Diesel, twin screw

The uncompleted hull of the cruise ship *Royal Majesty* passed into the ownership of Kvaerner in 1990, when they acquired the bankrupt Wartsila Masa Shipyard at Helsinki. Completed by the Norwegian-owned shipbuilder at its own expense, she was first chartered to Majesty Cruise Line, a Greek concern. The charter agreement contained provision for Majesty Cruise to purchase ten percent of the equity value of the ship. Subsequently, Norwegian Cruise Line purchased the ship outright, renaming her *Norwegian Majesty* and integrating her into their long-established cruise operations. This has left her as another one-off vessel but she offers a comparable standard of accommodation, shipboard facilities, and passenger service to other units of the fleet, cruising in the Caribbean and the other areas served by Norwegian Cruise Lines.

Norwegian Sea (1988-)

Owner: Norwegian Cruise Line—ex *Seaward* (1997)
Type: Active cruise ship—1,798 berths
Builder Wartsila A/B—Yard No 1294, floated November 14, 1987

ABOVE: Operating mainly in the Caribbean, *Norwegian Sea* has a four-star rating and offers affordable luxury to the 1,798 passengers that she can accomodate when fully loaded.

Dimensions: 42,276 GRT; 709 ft/216.2 m LOA; 105 ft/32.0 m BOA
Machinery: Diesel, twin screw

The *Norwegian Sea* makes an interesting comparison with the same fleet's *Norwegian Dream* and *Norwegian Wind,* for she is approximately of the size they were prior to the jumboization treatment they received between 1997 and 1998.

Completed as the *Seaward*, she was delivered on May 16, 1988. In a practice that has become increasingly popular throughout the 1990s, she was not christened officially until May 26, 1988, at New York, ten days after she was handed over to her owners and a significant time after she was first floated out of her building berth. She received her new name *Norwegian Sea* in 1997, when Norwegian Cruise Line invoked a general renaming program.

The *Norwegian Sea* makes predominantly Caribbean cruises. With a passenger space ratio of 28.1 she is, according to this yardstick, the least spacious of the Norwegian Cruise Line's fleet of ships. However, her four star grading for amenities and quality of service confirms her position as a vessel offering affordable cruises with a measure of added value.

The *Norwegian Sky*-class
Owner: Norwegian Cruise Line

Norwegian Sky (1999-)
ex *Costa Olympia* (1998)
Type: Active cruise ship—2,450 berths
Builder: Bremer Vulkan—Yard No 1108; completed by Lloyd Werft—Yard No 108
Dimensions: 77,104 GRT; 853 ft/260 m LOA; 105 ft/32.0 m BOA
Machinery: Diesel-electric, twin screw

Norwegian Sun (2001-)
Type: Cruise ship under construction—c. 2,450 berths
Builder: Lloyd Werft—Yard No 109

Dimensions: 80,000 GRT; 853 ft/260 m LOA; 105 ft/32.0 m BOA
Machinery: Diesel-electric, twin screw

Pending the delivery of the *Norwegian Sun* in August 2001, the *Norwegian Sky* is the largest vessel in the Norwegian Cruise Line fleet, now a subsidiary company of the Star Cruise AS Sendirian Berhad of Malaya. The ship started life as part of a two ship order for Costa Cruise Line, the first vessel, the *Costa Victoria* being completed and delivered to these owners as originally intended. However, her consort was only 40 percent complete when Bremer Vulkan were declared bankrupt and work on the ship ceased while the receiver endeavored to rescue the shipyard from its financial plight and deal with creditor's claims. Initially, Costa Cruise Line themselves sought to have the half completed *Costa Olympia* completed for them elsewhere, but this fell through after protracted but unresolved negotiations.

In the spring of 1997, the Norwegian Cruise Line signed a letter of intent to purchase the partly-built hull from the receiver for $28 million. In December 1997, the incomplete *Costa Olympia* was moved to the Lloyd Werft shipyard at Bremerhaven, which had been contracted to finish her, and, prior to completion, in a ceremony in February 1998, she was renamed *Norwegian Sky* to indicate her change of ownership.

Reflecting the different requirements of their respective owners, the *Norwegian Sky* and the *Costa Victoria*, though of broadly similar tonnage and comparable dimensions, are internally quite different. Reflecting the different sizes of their passenger complements, the *Costa Victoria* has a passenger space ratio of 39.0, slightly higher than the 38.0 of the *Norwegian Sky*. In other respects they are graded at about the same level. Norwegian Cruise lines offers affordable, middle of the range cruises suited to a broad cross-section of passenger clientele with itineraries that encompass all the principal destinations and circuits in Europe and the Americas, including to Hawaii.

The *Norwegian Sun*, started at the Aker Weft yard and then moved to the Lloyd Werft shipyard for completion after her launch may be regarded as a hybrid of the *Costa Victoria/Norwegian Sky* type but, ordered by Norwegian Cruise Line as a running mate for the *Norwegian Sky*, she is closer to her in configuration and in terms of accommodation standard and layout. She is scheduled to enter service in August 2001 with the possibility of another two ships of this category to follow a year or more later.

Ocean Princess
see the *Sun Princess*-class

Olympic (1911-1935)

Owner: White Star Line
Type: Former passenger liner—2,584, later reduced to 1,447, passengers in three classes
Builder: Harland & Wolff, Belfast—Yard No 400, launched October 20, 1910
Dimensions: 46,440 GRT; 882 ft/268.8 m LOA; 93 ft/28.2 m BOA
Machinery: Combined steam reciprocating and low pressure steam turbine, triple screw

The first of a trio of passenger liners of moderate speed but with exceptionally luxurious appointments, the *Olympic* entered the North Atlantic passenger trade on June 14, 1911 when she made her maiden departure from Southampton for New York. She was a well patronized ship, regarded affectionately by her regular passengers. Her later sisters *Titanic* and *Britannic* were sunk respectively on April 14, 1912 and November 21, 1916, the latter while serving as a World War I converted hospital ship. As if her class was somehow blighted by an ill omen, the *Olympic* too suffered no less than three collisions over the course of her career. On September 20, 1911 she collided with

ABOVE: The first *Olympic*-class ship to sail from Harland &
Wolff's works in Belfast, *Olympic* was beautifully appointed, but
seemed to labor under the same curse as her sister, *Titanic*. She
suffered three collisions before being broken up in 1935.

the cruiser HMS *Hawke* off the Isle of Wight and was
severely damaged. While serving as a World War I
troopship, on May 12, 1918, she was attacked by a
German U-boat that collided with her and sank.
Fifteen years later, on May 16, 1934, the *Olympic*
rammed and sank the Nantucket lightship, killing the
entire crew.

The *Olympic* benefited from a major reconstruction
in the wake of the *Titanic* disaster, improving her
watertight integrity and increasing substantially her
lifeboat provision. Further renovation after she was
returned to her owners at the end of World War I
included conversion to oil-fired boilers. Steady and
consistent service on the Atlantic run occupied the
next 14 years but, like the *Majestic* (ex *Bismarck*), she
did not survive for long after the amalgamation of the
Cunard and White Star companies. After a brief period of lay-up at her home port, she was disposed of for
scrap in October 1935.

Oriana (1960-1986)

Owner: P&O Line (previously Orient Line)
Type: Preserved former passenger liner
Builder: Vickers Armstrong, Barrow-in-Furness—
Yard No 1061, launched November 3, 1959
Dimensions: 41,925 GRT; 804 ft/245.1 m LOA;
97 ft/29.6 m BOA
Machinery: Steam turbines, twin screw

Ordered as an Orient Line ship, the striking *Oriana*
entered the express passenger and mail service to
Australia via Suez in December 1960. Her maiden
voyage became a round-the-world trip, for, following
her arrival at Sydney after crossing the Indian Ocean,
she continued to Auckland and ports on the west coast
of the United States before returning home via the

ABOVE RIGHT: The *Oriana*, which once plied the route between
Southampton and Sydney and is now a tourist attraction on the
Huangpo River in China.

RIGHT: Taking the name of her esteemed predecessor is the new
Oriana, which first took to the seas in 1994.

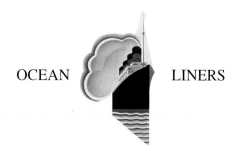

OCEAN LINERS

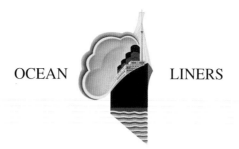

Panama Canal. Second only to the *Canberra* on the Australia run, the *Oriana* collaborated with the P&O ship in a joint service, which ensured regular departures from Southampton and Sydney.

The close working relationship between the Orient and P&O concerns was cemented in a total merger in 1965 with the formation of P&O-Orient Lines. By 1966, in recognition of the dominant partner in the combined company, it was restyled P&O Line. The *Oriana* continued on the scheduled service to Australasia, interspersed with occasional cruise excursions, until 1973. From that time she was adapted, like the *Canberra*, for full-time cruising. *Oriana* did not as readily adjust to her new role and it became inevitable that she would soon be disposed of as new purpose-built cruise ships were commissioned.

In 1986, she was sold to become a permanently moored hotel ship and tourist center at Beppu Bay, Kyushu, Japan from August 1, 1987. Eight years later the *Oriana* was sold again, for the same purpose, and moved to the River Huangpo in Shanghai, China. So successful has she been in her new role, that a share release has been announced, offering the Chinese public the opportunity to have a stake in her.

Oriana (1995-)

Owner: P&O Cruises
Type: Active cruise ship—2,108 berths
Builder: Meyer Werft, Papenburg—Yard No 636, floated July 1994
Dimensions: 69,153 GRT; 850 ft/259.1 m LOA; 105 ft/32 m BOA
Machinery: Diesel, twin screw

ABOVE LEFT: *Oriana*'s distinctive upper deck tails and the aft pool on Deck 8.

LEFT: *Oriana*'s Crow's Nest Bar.

RIGHT: Combining sleek modern design and the best of traditional ocean liners, the four-star accomodation available on *Oriana* is popular with P&O's customers.

Ordered on January 20, 1992 as P&O's first new ship for almost 30 years, the project for a large cruise ship for the British market had been under consideration by the company since 1988. The new ship's keel was laid on March 11, 1992, her construction taking three years to complete. Shortly after she was floated, she was towed down the River Ems to Emden in February 1995, to commence sea trials, still not officially named. Unfortunately, damage to her propellers was sustained in shallow water during the trials necessitating repairs before she could enter service and precipitating a problem that was to a come back and haunt the new vessel during her inaugural season.

The ship was christened *Oriana* by Her Majesty Queen Elizabeth at Southampton on April 6, 1995, reviving the name of her well-regarded predecessor which had retired just nine years earlier. The *Oriana*'s maiden cruise commenced on April 9, 1995, taking her to Madeira, the Canary Islands, Morocco, Gibraltar, and Portugal over 14 days, an itinerary she would continue to follow in the seasons ahead.

The *Oriana* is an elegant, tastefully decorated ship combining modern features and facilities with a traditional decor and ambience that evokes earlier eras of passenger travel at sea. A distinctive feature of her public space is the four-story high waterfall, centrally placed as the focal point of the atrium reception area. Of her 914 cabins, 594 are on the exterior of the ship although only 118 of these have private balconies, a lower ratio than might be anticipated given the aspirations of today's cruise vacationers. The *Oriana* is graded as four star superior along with the *Arcadia*, but her passenger space ratio at 37.8 is somewhat lower than the older vessel's 43.5. She continues to operate European cruises from her home port Southampton.

The vibration and other mechanical teething difficulties experienced by the *Oriana* were corrected later in her first season but she has suffered other problems since then. In 1999 a stern tube bearing failure occurred shortly after a major refit at Southampton which put her out of action for two weeks. On September 28, 2000 she was hit by a freak wave in the Atlantic when bound for Southampton. Windows were smashed, cabins flooded, and minor injuries were sustained by a number of passengers.

Pacific Sky (1984-)

Owner: P&O Holidays—ex *Sky Princess* (2000), ex *Fairsky* (1988)
Type: Active cruise ship—1,600 berths
Builder: Chantiers du Nord et de la Méditerranée, La Seyne—Yard No 1436, launched November 6, 1982
Dimensions: 46,087 GRT; 789 ft/240.5 m LOA; 92 ft/28.0 m BOA
Machinery: Steam turbines, twin screw

The last ship to be completed for Italy's Sitmar Shipping Line, the *Fairsky* was named at Los Angeles on May 5, 1984. Unusually, at a time when diesel engines were being selected as the prime mover for large cruise ships, the *Fairsky* had turbines installed making her one of the last, large, passenger steamships to be built.

She was employed in the United States market, cruising the West Coast. In 1988, she transferred to Princess Cruises as the *Sky Princess*, when P&O acquired the Sitmar operation, continuing with her Pacific coast cruise program. Twelve years later she was renamed a second time when transferred to the P&O Holidays company as the P&O Group's Australian based ship.

Under the name *Pacific Sky* she replaced the old *Fair Princess* (ex *Fairsea*, ex *Fairland*, ex *Carinthia*), her vacated place on the United States' circuit being filled by the *Regal Princess*. Specializing in cruises for Australasian market in Antipodean and Pacific waters, the *Pacific Sky* brings an elevated standard of accommodation and passenger amenities to her new role, offering substantially more commodious accommodation to this particular cruise market.

Paradise

see the *Fantasy*-class

Queen Elizabeth (1940-1972)

Owner: Cunard Line

Type: Former passenger liner—2,283 passengers in three classes

Builder: John Brown, Clydebank—Yard No 552, launched September 27, 1938

Dimensions: 83,675 GRT; 1,031 ft/314.3 m LOA; 118.4 ft/36.1 m BOA

Machinery: Steam turbines, quadruple screw

The largest British-built passenger liner and, arguably, the largest true passenger liner ever built, the *Queen Elizabeth* with her running mate *Queen Mary* established the Cunard Line as the dominant operator on the North Atlantic service. She was completed after the outbreak of World War II and thus commenced her

BELOW & OVERLEAF: The elegant and fast *Queen Elizabeth* was a highly effective troopship during World War II and sailed the transatlantic route for years after, until competition from airlines made her uneconomical to run.

long career as a fast troopship making her first, secret, sailing to New York on February 27, 1940. Because of their high speed both *Queen*s operated independently of convoys as this was considered to be their best form of defense against submarine attack. The *Queen Elizabeth* gave sterling auxiliary service, particularly on the "GI shuttle" in the build-up to D-Day. She established a record in the summer of 1944 for the greatest number of passengers ever carried by a single ship when she conveyed 15,200 American troops to Britain on one crossing. Between them, over their long period of wartime trooping, the *Queen Elizabeth* and *Queen Mary* carried two million servicemen and steamed a combined distance equivalent to 40 circumnavigations of the globe.

Prestige dictated that the *Queen Elizabeth* should receive preferential treatment in restoration for entry into peacetime passenger operations. Her first post-war sailing was made on October 16, 1946, just over six months after she had been returned to her owners. Thereafter she maintained a regular schedule of

18 round trip voyages every year broken only by routine dry-docking and maintenance. She never attempted to take the Atlantic Blue Riband from her consort.

As ocean liner traffic dwindled in the 1960s, the *Queen Elizabeth* became uneconomical to operate, on some voyages carrying more crew then fare-paying passengers. The end came in 1968, when Cunard sold her to a business consortium for retention as a hotel ship and convention center, berthed in Port Everglades. This soon fell through because of financial difficulties that beset her new owners and the prospect of scrapping loomed. Fortunately, this was averted when the Chinese shipping magnate C. Y. Tung purchased her in August 1970. Destined to become an international university of the sea, it seemed her fortunes had irreversibly turned for the better. Renamed the *Seawise University* and taken in hand for conversion at Hong Kong, fate was to deal her a final blow, for she was destroyed by fire on January 9, 1972, when virtually complete and ready to commence her new duties.

Queen Elizabeth 2 (1969-)

Owner: Cunard line

Type: Active converted passenger liner—1,877 berths

Builder: Upper Clyde Shipbuilders, Clydebank—Yard No 736, launched September 20, 1967

Dimensions: 70,327 GRT; 963 ft /293.6 m LOA; 105 ft/32 m BOA

Machinery: Diesel-electric, twin screw (Steam turbines, twin screw—as built)

As traditional ocean liner route passengers ebbed away in the 1960s and the earlier *Queen*s became more and more advanced in years, Cunard agonized over the best form that a replacement ship should take. They settled on a two-class dual role ship, comparable to Canadian Pacific's pre-war *Empress Of Britain*, maintaining a limited schedule of North Atlantic sailings in the summer months and spending the rest of the year on luxury cruises. Her excursions would include an annual round-the-world cruise.

In her style and appearance, the *Queen Elizabeth 2* broke a number of long held traditions, which was not well received by some of the more old-fashioned purists of the trade press and the public at large. A major criticism concerned the abandonment of Cunard's traditional crimson and black colors on her equally novel funnel. Furthermore, the *Queen Elizabeth 2*'s early years were dogged by mechanical problems, all of which served to fuel a rather negative attitude toward the new ship which lasted throughout her early career. Her maiden voyage, which was delayed, took place on May 2, 1969. Thereafter, the *Queen Elizabeth 2* settled into her routine and despite her early difficulties received the acceptance and the acclaim that she deserved. Nevertheless, after the *Queen Elizabeth 2* completed troopship duties in May 1982, in connection with the Falkland Islands dispute with Argentina, her owners took the opportunity to have her funnels discreetly repainted in the Cunard style, even though, temporarily, her hull was painted in an unusual shade of "Confederate" pale gray.

Although the *Queen Elizabeth 2* had slowly built up a following, trading off her superliner status and satisfying a niche market with scheduled Atlantic crossings and cruises, she was not a profitable vessel. A major factor influencing this was her steam turbine engines that were expensive to run as fuel costs escalated. The decision was made, therefore, to re-engine her with a diesel-electric power plant. Carried out between October 1986 and April 1987, this and other modifications, which included a broader, more attractive funnel, were intended to give the *Queen Elizabeth 2* a healthy life extension out into the foreseeable future. The recent announcement of a new Cunarder, the *Queen Mary 2*, due for delivery in 2003 may, however, mean that the *Queen Elizabeth 2*'s 30 plus year career is drawing to a close.

ABOVE RIGHT: The *QE2*'s controversial funnel, now painted in the traditional Cunard colors.

RIGHT & OVERLEAF: After initial criticism and public indifference, the *Queen Elizabeth 2* has become a popular and prestigious liner and completes transatlantic runs as well as luxury cruises.

Queen Mary (1936-1968)

Owner: Cunard Line

Type: Preserved former passenger liner—2,139, later reduced to 1,995, passengers in three classes

Builder: John Brown, Clydebank—Yard 534, launched September 26, 1934

Dimensions: 81,235 GRT; 1,019 ft/310.7 m LOA; 118 ft/36 m BOA

Machinery: Steam turbines, quadruple screw

Without question, the most famous British passenger liner ever built, the *Queen Mary* captured the nation's heart as the symbol of recovery from the ravages of the Great Depression during the 1930s. So severe were the downward spiraling economic forces at the time that the great liner's construction was suspended for nearly two and a half years. Work on her was only reactivated when Government loans were extended to the owners to help finance her completion on the condition that Cunard combined with the rival White Star concern to form one large North Atlantic operator under the Red ensign. Taking the name of the Queen consort, a significant departure from Cunard tradition, the *Queen Mary* entered service in May 1936 and soon showed herself to be a classic record breaking express liner. She took the *Normandie*'s Blue Riband honors with speeds of 30.14 knots westbound and 30.63 knots eastbound on her fifth round-voyage. In response, the *Normandie* clipped small margins off the *Queen Mary*'s crossing time, only for the British ship to establish new records in 1938 which remained unbroken until 1952: 30.99 knots eastbound and 31.69 knots westbound.

As the nation's mercantile flagship, the *Queen Mary* was extraordinarily popular and, unlike her French contemporary, she made a handsome profit for

BELOW: Friendly rival of the French *Normandie*, and one of the greatest liners ever launched, the *Queen Mary*.

ABOVE: Popular and profitable in service, the *Queen Mary*'s record-breaking crossing of the Atlantic stood for 14 years. Also in the photograph is the SR.N1, an early type of hovercraft.

her owners. An equally successful tour of duty as a World War II troopship was marred only by a collision accident on October 2, 1942. When northwest of the appropriately named Bloody Foreland, off northern Ireland, while executing zigzag maneuvers, the escorting cruiser HMS *Curacoa* came under the *Queen Mary*'s bows and was cut in two by the huge transport, steaming at full speed and unable to stop. The cruiser sank rapidly with the deaths of 364 men out of the 390-strong crew. The *Queen Mary*'s mangled bows were soon repaired and she soon returned to her vital troop carrying duties.

With her war service over, the *Queen Mary*'s restoration had to wait until after that of her younger consort had been completed. She made her first post-war sailing to New York on July 31, 1947. The 'fifties were boom years for the Cunard *Queen*s, yet from this high point the decline in the succeeding decade was just as extreme, leading to the retirement of the *Queen Mary* in October 1967. She was sold to the city of Long Beach, California, for preservation as a museum, hotel ship, and convention center, remaining there to this day, a memorial to the great age of the ocean liner.

The *Radiance Of The Seas*
("Project Vantage"-class)
Owner: Royal Caribbean Cruise Lines

Radiance Of The Seas (2001-)
Type: Active cruise ship
Builder: Meyer Werft—Yard No 655
Dimensions: 88,000 GRT
Machinery: Gas turbine—electric drive, twin propulsion units

Brilliance Of The Seas (2002-)
Type: Cruise ship under construction
Builder: Meyer Werft—Yard No 656
Dimensions: 88,000 GRT
Machinery: Gas turbine—electric drive, twin propulsion units

The *Radiance Of The Seas*, due to enter service in February 2001, launches a completely new class of cruise ship, the "Project Vantage" series for Royal Caribbean Cruise Lines. The second ship, *Brilliance Of The Seas*, is scheduled for completion in June 2002. Two more unnamed ships of the type have been ordered from the Meyer Werft shipyard in Papenburg with tentative delivery dates in 2003 and 2004. In terms of size and principal dimensions, these vessels

ABOVE: An artist's impression of *Radiance of the Seas*, due to enter service in February 2001.

BELOW: The grand staircase entrance to the lower dining room onboard *Radiance of the Seas*.

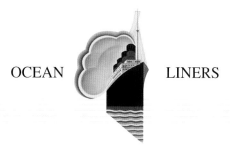

fall between the Vision-class ships and the giant "Project Eagle" class. They introduce the use of gas-turbine electric engines with podded propulsion units to the Royal Caribbean Cruise Line fleet.

Radisson Diamond (1992-)

Owner: Diamond Cruise Line
Type: Active cruise ship—354 passengers
Builder: Rauma Yards O/Y, Rauma—Yard No 310, launched June 20, 1991
Dimensions: 20,295 GRT; 423 ft/129.0 m LOA; 105 ft/32.0 m BOA
Machinery: Diesel, twin screw

Though small compared to the other ships described in this gazetteer, with many much bigger cruise vessels ranking in size between her and the next largest, the *Radisson Diamond* has been selected for inclusion because of her unusual character. Prior to its collapse in 1990, the Finnish shipyard Wartsila was the first to offer potential buyers a revolutionary cruise ship design based on the principles of the Small Waterplane Area Twin Hull (SWATH) configuration. Essentially, a

BELOW: The *Radisson Diamond* is a small ship but what she lacks in size she makes up for in style and quality of service, having been awarded no less that six stars.

catamaran craft, the main structure is suspended over two narrow flotation hulls each with a torpedo-shaped underwater form. The advantages of this type of vessel are reduced engine noise and vibration in the passenger areas, greater fuel efficiency, and enhanced stability in a seaway. The Wartsila concept was for a ship of around 44,000 gross tons, with principal dimensions of 534 feet LOA and 174 feet BOA. At one time it was suggested that the SWATH-ship hull form represented the way ahead for cruise ship design. In the event it fell to the Rauma shipyard in Finland to build the first, and, to date, only cruise ship of this type, being the *Radisson Diamond* completed in 1992 for the Diamond Cruise Line, now styled Radisson Seven Seas Cruises.

She entered service on April 30, 1992, cruising in the Caribbean and the Panama Canal area in winter and on the European circuit in summer. Her unusual shape is reflected in her dimensions which, being short but very wide still result in a gross tonnage of over 20,000. The beam to length ratio in her case is approximately 1.4, which compares to 1.7 for typical modern cruise ships with normal displacement hulls. Express passenger liners of the type designed specifically for the North Atlantic route had beam to length ratios as high as 1.9, revealing their extremely fine hull forms for very high speed.

The *Radisson Diamond* has a small passenger capacity for a ship of these proportions. Thus her passenger space ratio is a very high 57.3. With a six star rating from Fieldings, she is among the top cruise ships in the world for overall luxury, space, and quality of service. She has had one mishap during her nine years in service when she ran aground at Saxafjarden in the Stockholm archipelago after a power failure. Refloated after only a few hours, she had suffered only minor damage.

BELOW: Like her sister, the *Michelangelo*, the *Raffaello* was not destined to fulfill her intended role as a transatlantic liner but was instead sold to the Iranian Navy when trade steeply declined.

Raffaello (1965-1982)

Owner: Italia Line

Type: Former passenger liner—1,775 passengers in three classes

Builder: Cantieri Ruiniti dell'Adriatico, Trieste—Yard No 1864, launched March 24, 1963

Dimensions: 45,935 GRT; 905 ft/275.9 m LOA; 99 ft/30.2 m BOA

Machinery: Steam turbines, twin screw

The emergence of the *Raffaello* and *Michelangelo* on the Mediterranean route to New York in the mid-1960s was a reminder of the pre-war superliners *Rex* and *Conte Di Savoia*. But for the former pair, it was a matter of arriving too late, for the business was in serious decline and they sustained scheduled sailings for less than ten years, even then dependant on operating subsidies in order to maintain a viable service.

The *Raffaello* commenced her maiden voyage from Genoa to New York, following a shake-down cruise, on July 25, 1965. Her only mishap, in October 1966, was an engine fire that compelled a return to her home port, limping back there on one propeller. After a very brief period of full time cruising, when her regular service work had come to an abrupt and premature end, and a year and a half of inactivity, the *Raffaello* was sold for conversion into a crew accommodation ship for the Imperial Iranian Navy in February 1977. The Iranian flag was hoisted over her in August of that year when she took up her permanent berth at Bushire. Her accommodation was adjusted to permit 500 officers and 1,300 lower rank seamen and ratings to live aboard permanently.

The last that was reported of the former luxury liner *Raffaello* advised that she had been heavily damaged and set on fire by missiles launched in a Iraqi air attack in the early hours of November 21, 1982. Completely gutted and beyond recovery, reminiscent of the *Rex* and *Conte Di Savoia*, she was subsequently broken up.

Regal Princess

see the *Crown Princess*-class

Rembrandt (1959-)

Owner: Premier Cruises—ex *Rotterdam* (1997)

Type: Active converted passenger liner—1,114 berths

Builder: Rotterdam Drydock Co., Rotterdam—Yard No 300, launched September 13, 1958

Dimensions: 39,674 GRT; 748 ft/227.9 m LOA; 94 ft/29.7 m BOA

Machinery: Steam turbines, twin screw.

One of the most innovative passenger liners built for the North Atlantic service, the *Rotterdam* made her maiden voyage from Rotterdam to New York on September 3, 1959. Her near-aft placed engines vented through two narrow athwart-ships exhaust pipes, traditional funnels having been dispensed with altogether. Internally, her accommodation reflected the tasteful qualities of grandeur and style associated with all the vessels of the Holland-America Line, her original owners, matched by equally high standards of cabin service. One of her more unusual features was her inter-twining staircases connecting the passenger decks that permitted passengers of different classes to pass close by one another without accessing each other's spaces.

With the older *Nieuw Amsterdam*, built 20 years earlier, the *Rotterdam* continued in the Atlantic schedules until 1969, when she was switched to dedicated cruising. Along with Home Line's *Oceanic*, she was among the very few conventional scheduled service liners that made a successful transition to luxury cruise operations. Twenty-eight years later, on September 30, 1997, after almost three times as long cruising as she had spent on the Atlantic run, Holland-America finally and, it is believed reluctantly, disposed of the *Rotterdam*. Up to that point she had carried an estimated 1.2 million passengers on 975 line and cruise voyages. These included her celebrated three to four month Grand World cruises. She was acquired by Cruise Holdings, latterly Premier Cruises, for

ABOVE: *Rembrandt* in her heyday, when she was known as *Rotterdam* and berths aboard her were highly sought after. Today her fate is in the balance after 40 years of first class service.

continued cruising in the Mediterranean, renamed *Rembrandt* in recognition of her Dutch origins. Plans in 2000 to rename her *Big Red Boat IV* were luckily thwarted when Premier Cruises failed financially. On the other hand, this has left the 40-year-old ship with a most uncertain future.

Rex (1932-1944)

Owner: Italia Line

Type: Former passenger liner—2,258 passengers in three classes

Builder: Amsaldo SpA, Sestri Ponente—Yard No 296, launched August 1, 1931

Dimensions: 51,730 GRT; 880 ft/268.3 m LOA; 97 ft/29.5 m BOA

Machinery: Steam turbines, quadruple screw

Italy's only holder of the Atlantic Blue Riband, the *Rex* entered serviced on September 27, 1932, when she made her maiden sailing from Genoa to New York. Her first voyage turned into an inauspicious affair, however, for when off Gibraltar she suffered serious engine damage and was held up there for three days while repairs were carried out. The following August she redeemed herself when she made a record Atlantic crossing westbound at 28.92 knots. She never secured the eastbound honors.

Like her fleetmate *Conte Di Savoia*, the *Rex* was a stylishly appointed vessel, her public rooms decorated in the style of the Italian Roccoco. Taking advantage of the warmer temperatures of the southern route across the Atlantic, both ships featured a lido area on their open sun decks complete with outdoor swimming pools, amenities which were very rare on the passenger liners of those times. Throughout World War II, the *Rex* was laid up at Trieste, the Italian Navy having no use for her. In September 1944, the decision was made

ABOVE & LEFT: After an inauspicious maiden voyage during which she suffered mechanical failure, the *Rex* was a fast transatlantic liner and one of the few afloat at the time to boast an outdoor swimming pool.

to move the inactive liner to a place of shelter as the fighting in northern Italy intensified following Italy's surrender and as the Allies steadily advanced toward the retreating German Army. The move was not a wise one, though, for, fearful that an attempt might be made to block the port by sinking her at the entrance to Trieste, British aircraft attacked and sank her off Capo d'Istria on September 8, 1944 to prevent this from happening. Engulfed in flames, the wrecked *Rex* turned over on her beam ends and sank in shallow water. When salvage could be undertaken, it was considered that the badly damaged *Rex* was beyond recovery so, from 1947, she was scrapped where she lay, the difficult operation taking until the summer of 1958 to complete.

Rhapsody Of The Seas
see the *Legend Of The Seas*-class

The *Rotterdam*-class

Owner: Holland-America Line

Rotterdam (1997-)

Type: Active cruise ship—1,620 berths
Builder: Fincantieri, Marghera—Yard No 5980, launched December 21, 1996
Dimensions: 59,692 GRT; 781 ft/238.0 m LOA; 105 ft/32.0 m BOA
Machinery: Diesel-electric, twin screw

Amsterdam (2000-)

Type: Active cruise ship—1,600 berths
Builder: Fincantieri, Venice—Yard No. 6052
Dimensions: 60,874 GRT; 777 ft/237 m LOA; 105 ft/32 m BOA
Machinery: Diesel-electric, twin screw

The *Rotterdam* was scheduled to enter service on August 1, 1997, to mark Holland-America Line's 125th anniversary, but this was threatened by capacity pressures at the Fincantieri shipyards. As it turned out her commissioning was delayed until November 1997 denying her owners both the planned celebration and

the associated publicity. She inherited an illustrious name, being the sixth passenger vessel to bear it and benefiting from the enormous popularity of her immediate predecessor.

Constructed to some extent in parallel with the two similar-sized ships of the *Volendam* class, the *Rotterdam* and her sister *Amsterdam* offer a somewhat different slant in the style of their accommodation, plus greater spaciousness in a hull of comparable dimensions. Hence, this pair have, marginally, a higher space ratio of 45.1 compared with the 43.7 of the *Volendam* and *Zaandam*. Unlike the slightly bigger *Volendam* ships, the *Rotterdam* duo have a more formal and traditional design and are capable of deep water operation in comfort. Their twin athwart-ships-situated, thin tubular funnels may identify them.

All four ships are graded as five star by Fieldings and, as numerous cruise commentators report, these vessels offer in all respects "very polished cruises." Being the latest ship to join the Holland-America Line fleet, the *Amsterdam* is the culmination of a 16-year building program, comprising ten new ships, which has elevated the company to a position as one of the top operators in the industry. Another five, even larger, ships are now under construction. The *Amsterdam* opened her maiden season with a first sailing in October 2000.

Today, Holland-America is part of the huge Carnival Corporation group of companies. Projecting a reputation for high quality, earned during the line's days as a prominent North Atlantic operator, Holland-America cruise ships are selected by discerning travelers who prefer a little less "razzmatazz."

ABOVE RIGHT & RIGHT: The two ships of Holland-America's *Rotterdam*-class, *Rotterdam* (ABOVE) was launched in 1997, and *Amsterdam*, (BELOW) in 2000.

OCEAN LINERS

Royal Princess (1984-)

Owner: Princess Cruises
Type: Active cruise ship—1,260 berths
Builder: Wartsila A/B, Helsinki—Yard No 464, floated February 17, 1984
Dimensions: 44,588 GRT; 756 ft/230.6 m LOA; 106 ft/32.2 m BOA
Machinery: Diesel, twin screw

Following P&O's acquisition of Princess Cruises, the *Royal Princess* constituted the first evidence of the company's plans to expand and enhance this already popular fleet. Almost twice the size of the existing vessels of the "Love Boat" series, she was the first cruise ship to have an atrium, the now mandatory multi-deck open area in the center of cruise ships complete with waterfalls, glass-walled lifts, and live vegetation. The atrium on the *Royal Princess* was the brainchild of the Norwegian naval architect Njal Eide.

The *Royal Princess* was delivered to her owners on October 30, 1984, making her first call at Southampton where her naming ceremony took place on November 15. She then moved to Miami where she was based for Caribbean cruises, transferring to the Alaska circuit during the summer season. Establishing a quality of accommodation and service that have helped to elevate Princess Cruises to its current position as a leading cruise operator, the *Royal Princess* is graded as four star superior with a passenger space ratio of 36.9.

Ryndam
see the *Statendam*-class

Sea Princess
see the *Sun Princess*-class

BELOW: The *Royal Princess* is notable for being the first liner to have an atrium included in her design, an idea that has become widely copied throughout the industry.

Sensation
see the *Fantasy*-class

The *Seven Seas Mariner*-class
Owner: Radisson Seven Seas Cruises

Seven Seas Mariner (2001-)
Type: Active cruise ship—720 berths
Builder: Chantiers de L'Atlantique, St. Nazaire—Yard No K31
Dimensions: 46,500 GRT

Seven Seas Voyager (2003-)
Type: Cruise ship under construction—c. 720 berths
Builder: Mariotti SpA, Genoa
Dimensions: 46,500 GRT

The first of two larger, follow-on cruise ships for the Radisson Seven Seas company, broadly acknowledged as being the industry leader for quality and excellence, the *Seven Seas Mariner* is due to commence operations in March 2001. She joins, among other vessels, the *Seven Seas Navigator* (ex *Akademik Nikolay Pelyugin*), a ship started at the Admiralteiskiy shipyard, St. Petersburg, for Russian owners and completed for Radisson Seven Seas after her launch, on September 23, 1999, at the Mariotti yard in Genoa.

The *Seven Seas Navigator* is renowned for being the world's first all-suite cruise ship in keeping with her owners' philosophy of providing up-market, highly luxurious and spacious cruise comfort visiting some of the world's most exotic locations. The pair of imminent, larger ships will surpass even the *Seven Seas Navigator*, for they will be the world's first all suite/all balcony cruise vessels, the earlier ship's accommodation providing balconies for only 80 percent of the staterooms. Radisson prefer to talk in terms of guests rather than passengers for whom, aboard the *Seven Seas Mariner* and *Seven Seas Voyager*, there will be just 280 luxury suites each of a minimum area of 28 square meters. Aboard Radisson's existing ships, passenger space ratios are as high as 59.7 for the *Paul Gauguin* and 61.2 for the *Seven Seas Navigator*. It may be anticipated that passenger space aboard the new ships will be even higher and, with a fleet-wide six star rating from Fieldings, Radisson Seven Seas Cruises can only be described as "the best of all," focussed on a select clientele who are prepared to pay more for a truly high standard.

Mariotti have been selected as the builder of the second new ship, *Seven Seas Voyager*, but an order for a third ship of this exclusive configuration is expected to be placed with Chantiers de L'Atlantique. Unlike their predecessor, which was fitted with conventional screw propellers, Radisson's new pair will have podded propulsion units.

Radisson Seven Seas Cruises, as an operator of distinction, operates in less traditional cruise areas seeking out that "something different" for their customers. Itineraries are worldwide but embrace such places as Tahiti and other Polynesian islands, the Ligurian coast, and French Riviera in the Mediterranean and to Peru, Ecuador, and Chile off South America's west coast.

The *Sovereign Of The Seas*-class
Owner: Royal Caribbean Cruise Lines

Sovereign Of The Seas (1987-)
Type: Active cruise ship—2,600 berths
Builder: Chantiers de L'Atantique, St. Nazaire—Yard No A29, floated April 4, 1987
Dimensions: 73,192 GRT; 880 ft/268.3 m LOA; 105 ft/32.0 m BOA
Machinery: Diesel, twin screw

Monarch Of The Seas (1991-)
Type: Active cruise ship—2,764 berths
Builder: Chantiers de L'Atantique, St. Nazaire—Yard No A30, launched September 21, 1990
Dimensions: 73,941 GRT; 880 ft/268.3 m LOA; 105 ft/32.0 m BOA
Machinery: Diesel, twin screw

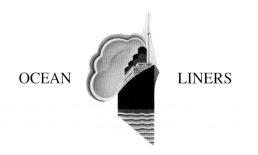

Majesty Of The Seas (1992-)

Type: Active cruise ship—2,766 berths
Builder: Chantiers de L'Atantique, St. Nazaire—Yard No B30, launched September 21, 1991
Dimensions: 73,937 GRT; 880 ft/268.3 m LOA; 105 ft/32.0 m BOA
Machinery: Diesel, twin screw

The *Sovereign Of The Seas*, the inaugural ship of Royal Caribbean's lead trio of 70,000 gross ton cruise ships, was another vessel that could claim the title of largest passenger ship in the world when she was completed in December 1987. She represented a huge growth in size of some 30 percent on the largest dedicated cruise ships then in service, almost as dramatic as the quantum leap in the scale of this type of ship that was made when her fleet-mate *Voyager of the Seas* emerged 12 years later.

Unlike the later "Project Vision" series, which have diesel-electric power plants, the *Sovereign*-class ships are geared motorships. Following the completion of acceptance trials, she was transferred to Miami where she was officially christened in a naming ceremony on January 15, 1988. An interlude of almost four years passed before the first of two sister-ships, the *Monarch Of The Seas*, joined her in October 1991. This was caused by a serious fire aboard the *Monarch*, which was started during welding operations on December 3, 1990, while she was fitting out. The fire destroyed a large section of the vessel, necessitating extensive repairs and delaying her scheduled completion by over six months.

Majesty Of The Seas was accepted from the builders just over a year later, completing this phase of Royal Caribbean's fleet-expansion program. Some six years later, on December 15, 1998, the *Monarch Of The Seas* struck a reef in Philipsburg Harbor on the island of St Maarten. Beached on soft sand, her 2,557 passengers were evacuated as a precautionary measure when the ship started to take water forward. Three days later, the *Monarch Of The Seas* was refloated and proceeded to Miami from where she was dispatched to Mobile, Texas, for repairs at the Atlantic Marine shipyard. The work involved the replacement of extensive amounts of steel work. She did not return to service until March 1999. Apart from the cost of the repairs and the lost cruise revenues, her owners faced additional financial liabilities in respect of the severe damage inflicted on the coral reef, an important diving site, which it was feared would adversely affect tourism to the island.

The *Sovereign Of The Seas*, along with the *Monarch* and *Majesty,* remain graded as moderate to superior in respect of the scope of their facilities and the level of service. Passenger space ratio at an average of 31.6 is now on the low size for ships of this size, indicating the extent to which advances in space allocation that have been made in the decade since they began cruising.

Splendour Of The Seas
see the *Legend Of The Seas*-class

The *Statendam*-class
Owner: Holland-America Line

Statendam (1993-)

Type: Active cruise ship—1,629 berths
Builder: Fincantieri—Yard No 5881
Dimensions: 55,451 GRT; 719 ft/219.2 m LOA; 102 ft/31 m BOA
Machinery: Diesel-electric, twin screw

Maasdam (1993-)

Type: Active cruise ship—1,629 berths
Builder: Fincantieri—Yard No 5882
Dimensions: 55,451 GRT; 719 ft/219.3 m LOA; 102 ft/31 m BOA
Machinery: Diesel-electric, twin screw

ABOVE, LEFT & RIGHT: Holland-America's reputation for excellence has been perpetuated by *Statendam* (ABOVE), *Maasdam* (LEFT), and *Ryndam* (RIGHT).

Ryndam (1994-)

Type: Active cruise ship—1,629 berths
Builder: Fincantieri—Yard No 5883
Dimensions: 55,451 GRT; 719 ft/219.3 m LOA;
102 ft/31 m BOA
Machinery: Diesel-electric, twin screw

Veendam (1996-)

Type: Active cruise ship—1,500 berths
Builder: Fincantieri, Venezia—Yard No 5954,
launched February 1996
Dimensions: 55,451 GRT; 719 ft/219.3 m LOA;
102 ft/31 m BOA
Machinery: Diesel-electric, twin screw

Precursors to the larger *Volendam* and *Rotterdam*-classes, the *Statendam* quartet were Holland-America's third generation of purpose-built cruise vessels, following on from the small *Prinsendam* and the later *Nieuw Amsterdam* and *Noordam* pair. Being of relatively moderate size by today's standards, this series of attractive ships perpetuates the Holland-America tradition for quality and elegance, serving a rather more up-market sector of the sea excursion business (so far they have elected not to build mega-cruise ships of the 100,000 ton plus category). This approach is reflected in the high passenger space ratios of the *Statendam*-class, at 48.3, and a superior grading in respect of the level of service and the range and standard of their passenger amenities.

The four *Statendam* ships serve a worldwide cruise circuit, all year round, their principal selling points being space, excellent passenger service, and a good measure of style as part of the highest-rated of the larger cruise fleets.

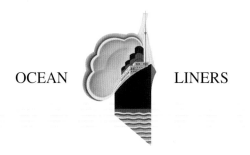

LEFT: *Veendam* completes the quartet of *Statendam*-class liners.

BELOW LEFT: Previously named *Song of America* and operated by Royal Caribbean Cruise Lines, the *Sunbird* has benefitted from a refit and now graces the Airtours fleet.

Sunbird (1982-)

Owner: Airtours Sun Cruises—ex *Song Of America* (1999)
Type: Active cruise ship—1,575 berths
Builder: Wartsila A/B, Helsinki—Yard No 431, floated November 26, 1981
Dimensions: 37,584 GRT; 704 ft/214.5 m LOA; 93 ft/28.4 m BOA
Machinery: Diesel, twin screw

As one of the first of the second generation of purpose-designed cruise ships that came onstream in the 1980s, the former *Song Of America* reflects the vertical division philosophy in the layout of her accommodation that was then in vogue. This placed cabins in the forward part of the ship, away from machinery noise and vibration, with public rooms located aft on the same decks. Today, the trend is for a form of horizontal division in which the whole of each deck is allocated to either cabins or for passenger amenities.

The *Song Of America* joined Royal Caribbean Cruise Lines, her original owners, on November 9, 1982, making her maiden voyage on December 5, of the same year. She was an upgraded version of the company's *Song Of Norway* trio of ships introduced between 1970 and 1972, of which the first two were subsequently stretched. Like all of the company's ships built since that time, the *Song Of America* carried the distinctive Viking Lounge, constructed in a lofty position around her funnel structure.

The *Song Of America* passed into Airtours ownership in 1999, renamed *Sunbird*, embarking on their program of low budget European and Caribbean cruises following a comprehensive refit at Cammell Laird. She is the highest rated of the Airtours Sun Cruises four ships, graded as moderate four star with a space ratio of 36.8. Airtours Sun Cruises has aimed their cruise products aboard the *Sunbird*, and their other ships, at the first-time cruise-maker. Cuisine, accommodation, and entertainment correspond to a typical holiday-package standard but represent exceptional value for money.

The *Sun Princess*-class
Owner: Princess Cruises

Sun Princess (1995-)
Type: Active cruise ship—2,272 berths
Builder: Fincantieri—Yard No 5909
Dimensions: 77,441 GRT; 856 ft/261.0 m LOA; 105 ft/32.0 m BOA
Machinery: Diesel-electric, twin screw

Dawn Princess (1997-)
Type: Active cruise ship—2,272 berths
Builder: Fincantieri
Dimensions: 77,441 GRT; 856 ft/261.0 m LOA; 105 ft/32.0 m BOA
Machinery: Diesel-electric, twin screw

Sea Princess (1998-)
Type: Active cruise ship—2,185 berths
Builder: Fincantieri, Monfalcone—Yard No 5998
Dimensions: 77,441 GRT; 856 ft/261.0 m LOA; 105 ft/32.0 m BOA
Machinery: Diesel-electric, twin screw

Ocean Princess (1999-)
Type: Active cruise ship—2,200 berths
Builder: Fincantieri—Yard No 6044, launched April 29, 1999
Dimensions: 77,441 GRT; 856 ft/261.0 m LOA; 105 ft/32.0 m BOA
Machinery: Diesel-electric, twin screw

The second phase of P&O's massive regeneration program for Princess Cruises, launched just over a decade ago, resulted in four similar but larger vessels of the *Crown Princess* type, essentially inherited from Sitmar, which constitute a unique sub-class. When she entered service at the end of 1995, the *Sun Princess* was the world's largest cruise ship, albeit for only a brief period for even bigger ships were commissioned within a year of her completion.

Recognizing that passenger aspirations were to have more and larger outside cabins with private balconies, the design of the *Sun Princess*-class reflects this requirement, providing over 40 percent of the accommodation in this form with a further 20 percent lacking balconies but still located on the outside of the hull. A wide variety of dining and entertainment tastes have been catered for and each of the ships feature open atriums, which lend a sense of space and brightness to their interiors. Indeed, the *Sun Princess*-class vessels have two such areas, the main facility being a four-deck high version with glass lifts, a waterfall, and full-size palm trees.

Sun Princess, Dawn Princess, Sea Princess, and *Ocean Princess*, the last of the group which entered service in February 2000, cruise in the Caribbean until the early summer when they transfer to Alaskan waters, based in California or Vancouver. These ships are graded either five star or four star superior with passenger space ratios of 39.4.

The *Superstar Leo*-class
Owner: Star Cruises AS Sendirian Berhad

Superstar Leo (1998-)
Type: Active cruise ship—3,350 berths
Builder: Meyer Werft, Papenburg—Yard No 646
Dimensions: 75,388 GRT; 879 ft/268.0 m LOA; 105 ft/32.0 m BOA
Machinery: Diesel-electric, twin screw

ABOVE: *Superstar Virgo* visits spectacular locations in South East Asia.

RIGHT: *Virgo*'s relaxing Taverna.

LEFT: *Superstar Leo*, which, like her sister, offers very high standards in everything from space ratios to cuisine.

Superstar Virgo (1999-)

Type: Active cruise ship—3,350 berths
Builder: Meyer Werft, Papenburg—Yard No 647
Dimensions: 75,338 GRT; 879 ft/268.0 m LOA; 105 ft/32.0 m BOA
Machinery: Diesel-electric, twin screw

This impressive pair of stylish, large cruise ships have been targeted at the growing Oriental market, based at Singapore and providing cruise excursions throughout South East Asia but primarily short cruises around the Malaysian peninsular. Although distinctly Eastern in style and flavor, European and other regional tastes are catered for aboard both ships and their schedules are organized to fit in conveniently with passenger arrivals by aircraft from Europe and the United States.

The recent down-turn in the fortunes of Pacific-rim economies has not hampered Star Cruises' ambition to develop into one of the leading cruise operating companies and the *Superstar Leo* and *Superstar Virgo* are evidence that these plans are well on their way to fruition. Four even larger vessels, two each of the *Libra* and *Sagittarius II* types, are scheduled to join them by 2004, increasing total passenger capacity to well in excess of 12,000 berths.

Accommodation and onboard facilities are to a very high standard, the public rooms and restaurants offering the choice of a variety of Oriental, European, and North American styles rather than the bland regionless "International" decor and cuisine exhibited on many of the modern cruise ships presently in service. An attempt has been made in some areas to recreate the glamor and ambience of the luxury liners of the pre-War era, with elegant decorations and design features that avoid tasteless excesses. It can be concluded that Star Cruises are focussing their operation on relaxation, with the "buzz" of the cruise experience gained from visits to locations where the scenery is uniquely spectacular coupled with first rate onboard service and a stimulating ambience that does not depend on frenetic exuberance for thrills.

LEFT: *Superstar Leo* and *Virgo* have been such great successes in South East Asia that their owner, Star Cruises, are planning a further four vessels even bigger vessels. This picture shows the Grand Piazza on *Superstar Virgo*.

ABOVE RIGHT: The inviting Parthenon pool with its Classical-inspired decor.

RIGHT: *Superstar Virgo*'s Promenade Deck.

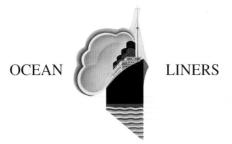

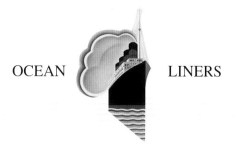

Titanic (1912-1912)

Owner: White Star Line

Type: Former passenger liner—2,603 passengers in three classes

Builder: Harland & Wolff, Belfast—Yard No 401, launched May 31, 1911

Dimensions: 46,329 GRT; 883 ft/269.2 m LOA; 93 ft/28.2 m BOA

Machinery: Combined triple expansion steam reciprocating and low pressure turbine, triple screw

Probably the most famous passenger liner ever, for all the worst possible reasons, the so-called "unsinkable" *Titanic* did not survive her maiden voyage which commenced on April 10, 1912. She sailed from Southampton bound for New York, with a complement of 1,308 passengers and 898 crew. Four days out, after calls at Cherbourg and Cobh, the *Titanic* collided with a massive iceberg which sliced a 300 ft long gash in her side. The liner had been designed to a three compartment standard of safety, meaning that she would remain afloat even if any three adjacent water-tight compartments were flooded. Regrettably, the extreme damage the *Titanic* had sustained had opened up five compartments to the inrush from the freezing ocean and from the moment of impact her fate had been irreversibly sealed. Inadequate life-saving facilities and an absence of other ships in close enough proximity to save all aboard her, resulted in the deaths of 1,503 persons, the majority of them immigrant passengers from third-class, including many women and children casualties. Ever since, the *Titanic* disaster

LEFT & INSET: The grand *Titanic* was the pride of the White Star fleet and the largest passenger liner afloat until her tragic meeting with an iceberg.

has become, metaphorically, a symbol representative of human folly and arrogance applied to all manner of situations, the majority having no connection whatsoever with the sea.

However, if it is possible for such a terrible catastrophe to have a positive outcome, the *Titanic*'s legacy has been the Safety of Life at Sea (SOLAS) regulations that have been in force since the time of her loss. Setting minimum standards of provision of life-saving and radio communication equipment, rules for distress calls, improved standards of crew training, and a winter-time ice patrol among many other measures the SOLAS regulations have helped to make ocean voyages safer for passengers and crews alike.

United States (1952-)

Owner: United States Lines, until 1969
Type: Idle passenger liner—1,928 passengers in three classes
Builder: Newport News Shipbuilding & Drydock Co., Virginia—Yard No 488, launched June 23, 1951
Dimensions: 53,329 GRT; 990 ft/301.8 m LOA; 101 ft/30.8 m BOA
Machinery: Steam turbines, quadruple screw

The *United States* was the fastest passenger liner ever built, although her outstanding success owed much to the fact that she was conceived, designed, and partially funded as an emergency high-speed naval transport for the United States Navy. Nevertheless, this should not detract from her achievements—unbroken record speeds across the Atlantic of 34.51 knots westbound and 35.59 knots eastbound—as well as her stylish modern appearance and luxuriously appointed interiors, every bit a classic ocean passenger liner. The extent of the *United States*' margin of supremacy was later reinforced, when relaxed security restrictions permitted the declaration that her maximum achieved speed was a staggering 38.3 knots, equivalent to almost 45 miles per hour.

Sustained by operating subsidies, the *United States* maintained a regular schedule of sailings between New York, Southampton, and Bremerhaven for 17 years. Consideration was given at one point to constructing a sister ship but after her smaller fleetmate *America* was sold in 1964, the *United States* was left as a lone vessel operating under the United States Lines banner. Later, as the fortunes of the Atlantic passenger trade continued to decline as the 1960s advanced, the United States Congress voted to terminate her Government funding from November 1969, precipitating an immediate end to her North Atlantic career.

Plans to convert the *United States* into a hospital ship, for attachment to the United States Rapid Deployment Force, and then into a luxury cruise ship both fell through and the slowly deteriorating ship has languished for the last 31 years with an increasingly uncertain future. After years tied up at a Norfolk, Virginia pier she made two further crossings of the Atlantic, neither under her own steam—eastward in 1992, bound for Tuzla, Turkey, where it was planned to renovate her, and then back to the United States when nothing came of this. The dilapidated ship, on which no work had been carried out, passed through the Dardanelles on June 18, 1996, at the start of the return crossing, under tow of the *Smit New York*. Bound for Philadelphia, where she arrived on July 23, 1996, she has remained berthed at a quay there since that time, the subject of at least one auction even though each sale has done nothing to end her protracted idleness. Realistically now, any chance of reactivating the *United States* as a revenue-earning ship has completely evaporated and the best that can be expected is that she may be renovated for preservation as a museum ship.

ABOVE RIGHT & RIGHT: The fastest passenger liner ever seen, the proud and elegantly appointed *United States* has been slowly rotting at berth for over 30 years at various berths.

OCEAN LINERS

Veendam
see the *Statendam*-class

Vision Of The Seas
see the *Legend Of The Seas*-class

The *Volendam*-class
Owner: Holland-America Line

Volendam (1999-)
Type: Active cruise ship—1,824 berths
Builder: Fincantieri, Marghera—Yard No 6035
Dimensions: 60,906 GRT; 777 ft/237.0 m LOA; 105 ft/32.0 m BOA
Machinery: Diesel-electric, twin screw

Zaandam (2000-)
Type: Active cruise ship—1,824 berths
Builder: Fincantieri, Marghera—Yard No 6036
Dimensions: 60,906 GRT; 777 ft/237.0 m LOA; 105 ft/32.0 m BOA
Machinery: Diesel-electric, twin screw

With the exception of the new *Amsterdam*, these Italian-built cruise ships are the latest to join the Holland-America Line fleet, representing a development in both size and amenities on the previous *Statendam*-class ships. With the *Rotterdam* and the *Amsterdam*, they are the culmination of a 16 year building program, comprising ten new purpose-built ships, which has elevated the company to a position as one of the top operators in the industry with a capacity of more than 13,000 berths. Another five ships now under construction will be even larger.

The *Volendam* entered service in October 1999, and the *Zaandam* made her debut in February of the following year, both delayed as a consequence of over-capacity at the Fincantieri yards—a measure of this shipbuilder's success at securing new construction orders.

Holland-America is now part of the huge Carnival Corporation group of companies. Projecting a reputation for high quality accommodation and service, established during the company's days as a prominent North Atlantic route operator, Holland-America cruise ships, including this trio, are graded at the top end of the scale and, with space ratios on the larger ships of the order of 44.4, they offer generous passenger space as a key selling factor. They tend to be selected by the more reflective traveler who prefers rather less of the "razzmatazz." Holland-America operates cruises to worldwide destinations embracing all the main circuits.

The *Voyager of the Seas*
(Project Eagle-class)
Owner: Royal Caribbean Cruise Line

Voyager of the Seas (1999-)
Type: Active cruise ship—3,840 berths
Builder: Kvaerner Masa, Turku—Yard No 1344, launched October 20, 1998
Dimensions: 137,296 GRT; 1,020 ft/311.0 m LOA; 128 ft/39.0 m BOA
Machinery: Diesel-electric, triple screw

Explorer Of The Seas (2000-)
Type: Active cruise ship—3,840 berths
Builder: Kvaerner Masa, Turku—Yard No 1345
Dimensions: 137,308 GRT; 1,020 ft/311.0 m LOA; 128 ft/39.0 m BOA
Machinery: Diesel-electric, triple screw

Adventure Of The Seas (2002-)
Type: Cruise ship under construction—3,840 berths
Builder: Kvaerner Masa—Yard No 1346
Dimensions: 137,300 GRT; 1,020 ft/311.0 m LOA; 128 ft/39.0 m BOA
Machinery: Diesel-electric, triple screw

ABOVE LEFT & LEFT: The two *Volendam*-class ships, *Volendam* (ABOVE LEFT) and *Zaandam* (LEFT) extend refined amenities to passengers who prefer a quieter cruise.

ABOVE & LEFT: The impressive *Explorer of the Seas* is the second ship in her class and can accomodate up to 3,840 passengers as can her older sister *Voyager of the Seas*.

The largest passenger ships in the world, for now at least, the *Voyager Of The Seas*-class took cruise vessel design to epic proportions, representing a huge increment of growth, of almost 40 percent over the then largest ships, the *Carnival Destiny* and *Carnival Triumph*. Among the many exciting design features of the *Voyager Of The Seas* (first of the "Project Eagle" series ships, as they have been dubbed, whose public spaces rival any of the contemporary, competitive cruise ships) are all the typical interior facilities, now fitted almost as standard, plus a number of new groundbreaking innovations. She has a five-deck high theater based on La Scala, Milan, and an ice-skating rink, the first to be installed on an ocean-going ship.

Based at Miami, serving the Caribbean circuit, the upgrading of the passenger-handling arrangements ashore was dictated by the introduction of such immense vessels. Hence, a new 250,000 square foot terminal has been commissioned by the Port Authority specially to accommodate the *Voyager*-class ships and other, future cruise vessels of this magnitude.

The passenger space ration of the *Voyager of the Seas* is not known but it can be expected to be considerably higher than the average figure in the upper 30s applicable to the other modern cruise ships of the Royal Caribbean Cruise Lines fleet.

The *Voyager of the Seas* entered service in November 1999, followed by the *Explorer Of The Seas* in October 2000. The latter vessel made a brief call at Southampton prior to heading off for her operational base, becoming the largest passenger ship to enter Britain's premier passenger port. The *Adventure Of The Seas*, third of what has grown into a five-ship class is scheduled for delivery in April 2002 with the fourth and fifth ships following in late 2002 and 2003.

Westerdam (1986-)

Owner: Holland-America Line—ex *Homeric* (1988)
Type: Active cruise ships—1,773 berths
Builder: Meyer Werft, Papenburg—Yard No 610, launched September 28, 1985
Dimensions: 42,092 GRT; 669 ft/204 m LOA; 95 ft/29.0 m BOA—as built
53,872 GRT; 798 ft/243.2 m LOA; 95 ft/29 m BOA—as stretched
Machinery: Diesel, twin screw

Ordered by the old Home Line company prior to its demise, the *Homeric*, as she was then known, holds a unique distinction in being the only large passenger ship to be launched beam on since Brunel's *Great Eastern* back in 1858. Unlike that faltering, snail's pace affair of the Victorian era, the *Homeric*'s launch in 1985 was a fast-moving spectacular event. Following builders' trials later that year, she entered service on May 6, 1986, cruising in the summer months from New York to Bermuda recalling the

ABOVE LEFT: *Westerdam*'s unusual and spectacular launch in 1985, when she was known as the *Homeric*.

ABOVE & LEFT: Now operated by the Holland-America Line *Westerdam* remains in active service.

pre-War "Millionaire's Cruise Ships," as they were called, the *Queen Of Bermuda* and *Monarch Of Bermuda* of Furness Withy. During the winter she worked in the Caribbean.

Holland-America Line purchased the *Homeric* in April 1988, taking delivery on November 27, 1988, and renaming her *Westerdam*, a name previously carried by a much smaller cargo passenger liner completed in 1948. On October 30, 1989, shortly after the Carnival Corporation absorbed Holland-America, the company returned the *Westerdam* to the shipyard for lengthening. She returned to service on completion of

the work on March 12, 1990, some 25 percent larger than her original size. The *Westerdam* remains an active unit of the Holland-America fleet being their third oldest vessel, predated by the *Nieuw Amsterdam* and *Noordam,* commissioned in 1983-1984. With the influx of the many new, state-of-the-art luxury cruise ships, though, it can only be a matter of time before Holland-America disposes of these three older vessels.

Zaandam
see the *Volendam*-class

Zenith
see the *Horizon*-class

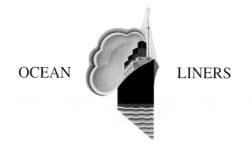

The Future

At the beginning of 2001 the international cruise ship industry is enjoying an unprecedented peak of business. More persons than ever before are taking a cruise holiday and, to satisfy this increasing level of demand, orders for cruise ships are at an all time high. Apart from the many new buildings already identified in the preceding passages, many other advanced cruise ships are under construction, the total number of vessels due to enter service over the next three to four years currently standing at fifty-one. At the same time, a variety of projects for revolutionary or extreme vessels are being promoted. Although these concept ships are not yet the subject of firm orders and may, in some cases, never be realized, they are nevertheless important as an innovative and influential force on future shipboard design features and accommodation trends, very much the life-blood of this vibrant industry.

Among the other new cruise ships currently under construction are the following named vessels:

BELOW: *The World of Residensea.*

Carnival Spirit

Owner: Carnival
Builder: Kvaerner Masa—Yard No 499
GRT: 84,000; **ft/m**: 958/292
Due into service: March 2001

Superstar Libra

Owner: Star
Builder: Meyer Werft—Yard No 648
GRT: 91,000; **ft/m**: 968/295.0
Due into service: August 2001

European Dream

Owner: Festival
Builder: Chantiers de L'Atlantique—Yard No V31
GRT: 58,500; **ft/m**: 823/251.0
Due into service: 2001

Carnival Pride

Owner: Carnival
Builder: Kvaerner Masa—Yard No 500
GRT: 84,000; **ft/m**: 958/292.0
Due into service: 2001

The World Of Residensea

Owner: ResidenSea
Builder: Fosen—Yard No 71
GRT: 40,000; **ft/m**: 643/196.0
Due into service: 2001

Carnival Legend

Owner: Carnival
Builder: Kvaerner Masa—Yard No 501
GRT: 84,000; **ft/m**: 958/292.0
Due into service: 2002

Coral Princess

Owner: Princess
Builder: Chantiers de L'Atlantique
GRT: 88,000; **ft/m**: ?
Due into service: 2002

European Vision

Owner: Festival
Builder: Chantiers de L'Atlantique—Yard No X31
GRT: 58,500; **ft/m**: 823/251.0
Due into service: 2002

Superstar Scorpio

Owner: Star
Builder: Meyer Werft—Yard No 649
GRT: 91,000; **ft/m**: 968/295.0
Due into service: 2002

Carnival Miracle

Owner: Carnival
Builder: Kvaerner Masa
GRT: 84,000; **ft/m**: 958/292.0
Due into service: 2003

Diamond Princess

Owner: Princess
Builder: Mitsubishi H.I.
GRT: 113,000; **ft/m**: 951/290.0
Due into service: 2003

Island Princess

Owner: Princess
Builder: Chantiers de L'Atlantique
GRT: 88,000; **ft/m**: ?
Due into service: 2003

"Project America" I

Owner: American Classic Voyages
Builder: Ingalls—Yard No 7671
GRT: 72,000; **ft/m**: 840/256.0
Due into service: 2003

Queen Mary 2

Owner: Cunard
Builder: Chantiers de L'Atlantique
GRT: 150,000; **ft/m**: 1,132/350.6
Due into service: 2003

Superstar Sagittarius II

Owner: Star
Builder: Meyer Werft
GRT: 110,000; **ft/m**: 1,037/316.0
Due into service: 2003

"Project America" II

Owner: American Classic Voyages
Builder: Ingalls—Yard No 7672
GRT: 72,000; **ft/m**: 840/256.0
Due into service: 2004

Sapphire Princess

Owner: Princess
Builder: Mitsubishi H.I.
GRT: 113,000; **ft/m**: 951/290.0
Due into service: 2004

Superstar Capricorn II

Owner: Star
Builder: Meyer Werft
GRT: 110,00; **ft/m**: 1,037/316.0
Due into service: 2004

Carnival Valor

Owner: Carnival
Builder: Fincantieri
GRT: 110,000

Of these new-buildings, one or two of the more interesting are worthy of greater mention here:

Following its acquisition by Carnival Corporation in May 1998 and the injection of new finance, Cunard Line, one of the two longest-established passenger shipping concerns still trading (the other, P&O, is also of British origin), has announced the placement of the order with Chantiers et Ateliers de L'Atlantique at St. Nazaire for a massive new ship. Similar in concept to the *Queen Elizabeth 2*, serving both the luxury cruise business and offering occasional transatlantic voyages, the name *Queen Mary 2* has been declared as the intended identity of the new vessel. Although her gross tonnage is only slightly greater at 150,000 tons than the largest cruise ships now in service, she will be significantly longer. Indeed, she will be among the first ships to exceed the length of the *Norway* (ex *France*) which has held this record for the past forty years. In her case, the record will be smashed by an increase of almost 100 feet.

Among the projected ships that may one day serve the burgeoning cruise industry is one which has been on the drawing board for some years. This is the *Phoenix World City* or *World City America* as it is alternatively named, the conception of Knut Kloster. On the scale of the immense Tourist-class, so-called "Cafeteria-ships" proposed for the North Atlantic run in the 1950's, the radical Kloster scheme calls for a type of apartment-suite vessel. This would feature passenger accommodation in tower blocks mounted on the main deck, each offset in such a way that the balconies of all apartments would face the ocean in at least one direction. With a tonnage of over 250,000 on an overall length of 1,250 feet (381.1 metres), not even the *Queen Mary 2* comes close to the scale of this mammoth vessel. The apartments of this colossus would be marketed on a time-share basis, in the same fashion as those as onshore resorts.

Interestingly, another Kloster scheme sponsored by a younger generation of the Kloster family, is set to become reality and features the *Phoenix World City* occupancy philosophy, albeit in a scaled down form. This is the *World Of Residensea*, now building in Norway and due to enter service in late 2001. Originally conceived as an 80,000 gross ton cruise ship, it is now only half that size. However, at the time that construction on her was commencing, it was revealed that over 60 percent of her timeshare apartments had already been sold.

Index of

Acknowledgments

The publisher wishes to thank the following for kindly supplying the images for this book:

Malcolm Fife for front cover and pages 2, 26-27, 30-31, 34 (top and bottom), 35 (bottom), 66-67 and 73 (bottom);
Thomson Cruises for pages 6-7 and 33 (top and bottom);
© Bettmann/CORBIS for running header on page 8 (top) and throughout book, and for pages 14-15, 17, 22, 29, 52 (bottom) and 94 (top and bottom);
© Steve Schimmelman/Windstar Cruises for page 8 (bottom);
© David Lees/CORBIS for pages 9, 11, 16, 23, 32 (bottom), 62 (bottom) and 131 (top);
© David Lyons/Event Horizons for pages 10, 44-45, 68 (top), 84 and 136 (bottom);
© CORBIS for pages 12, 13, 21 and 24 (top);
© Hulton-Deutsch Collection/CORBIS for pages 18, 19, 28, 40, 50, 92 and 96 (bottom);
© Christie's Images/CORBIS for page 20;
David L. Williams for pages 24 (bottom), 43 (bottom), 52 (top), 54 (bottom), 63, 65 (top), 72, 73 (top), 77 (top), 83 (top), 83 (bottom), 88 (bottom), 90 (bottom), 93 (top), 97, 100, 103, 124, 147 (inset), 149 (top and bottom) and 152 (bottom);
© The Mariners' Museum/CORBIS for pages 25 and 131 (bottom);
© Tim Wright/CORBIS for page 32 (top);
Roy J. Westlake, ARPS, for page 35 (top) and back cover;
John Blay for pages 36-37, 48-49, 75, 104 (bottom), 113 (bottom) and 122-123;
Alex Duncan for pages 42 and 134;
P&O Cruises for pages 43 (top), 46 (bottom left and right) and 115;
R. H. Bacon for pages 46 (top), 54 (top), 81 and 114 (top and bottom);
© Bob Krist/CORBIS for page 51;
Blohm & Voss for page 53;
Harland & Wolff for pages 56-57;
Carnival Cruises for pages 58-59, 78 and 79;
Celebrity Cruises for pages 60 (top left and right) and 85 (top and bottom);
Mr A. C. Novelli for pages 60 (bottom), 74 , 140 (bottom) and 142;

Cantieri Riuniti dell' Adriatico for page 62 (top);
© ATM Images for pages 65 (bottom) and 71;
N. V. Rollinson for pages 68 (bottom), 90 (top), 126-127 (main) and 155;
P&O Princess Cruises for page 70 (top and bottom);
Tom Rayner for pages 77 (bottom), 91 and 112;
Royal Caribbean International for pages 88 (top), 89, 126 (top and bottom left) and 152 (top);
Bettina Rohbrecht for page 93 (bottom);
Edward Bearman for page 96 (top);
Alstom – Chantiers de l'Atlantique for page 99;
© Buddy Mays/CORBIS for page 101;
Philip Rentell for pages 86 and 102;
Norwegian Cruise Line for pages 105, 106, 107, 108, 109 and 110 (top and bottom);
© R. Whitelaw for pages 113 (top) and 104 (top);
Mr G. Parrish for pages 117 and 118-119;
Cunard Line for page 121 (top and bottom);
GKN Westland Aerospace for page 125;
Italia Line for page 128;
© Jan Butchofsky-Houser/CORBIS for page 130;
Holland America Line for pages 133 (top and bottom), 138 (top and bottom), 139, 140 (top) and 154 (bottom);
Radisson Seven Seas Cruises for page 136 (top);
Star Cruises for pages 143 (top and bottom), 144 and 145 (top and bottom);
© Ralph White/CORBIS for pages 146-147 (main);
Holland America Line/Andy Newman for page 150 (top and bottom);
Meyer Werft for page 154 (top);
ResidenSea for page 156.
Special thanks to David L. Williams for all his help with illustrations, and to all the cruise companies whose assistance made this book possible.